TO KNOW GOD

A 5-DAY PLAN

TO KNOW GOD

A 5-DAY PLAN

MORRIS VENDEN

Review and Herald Publishing Association
Washington, DC 20039-0555
Hagerstown, MD 21740

This book was
Edited by Raymond H. Woolsey
Designed by Richard Steadham
Cover art by Richard Steadham
Type set: 10/11 Times Roman

PRINTED IN U.S.A.

Verses marked T.L.B. are taken from *The Living Bible*, copyright 1971 by Tyndale House
Publishers, Wheaton, Ill. Used by permission.

Bible texts credited to T.E.V. are from the *Good News Bible*—Old Testament: Copyright ©
American Bible Society 1976; New Testament: Copyright © American Bible Society 1966,
1971, 1976.

Library of Congress Cataloging in Publication Data

Venden, Morris L.
    To know God.

    1. Christian life—Seventh-day Adventist authors.
I. Title.
BV4501.2.V393 1983   248.4'8673   83-13755

ISBN 0-8280-0220-7

DAY 1

God is love. But how can I be sure? How can I know what He's really like?

Why do I need God, anyway? I'm really not such a bad person . . .

DAY 2

What are the steps in coming to Christ? How can I know whether I am saved?

How can I become personally acquainted with a God whom I can't see or hear?

DAY 3

Will the relationship with God go sour if I miss a day or two of communication?

How can I still have faith in Him when everything is going wrong at once?

DAY 4

Obedience. How? Why? And what happens when I fail?

Which comes first, victory or peace? How can I keep from sinning?

DAY 5

Christian growth. From baby Christian to maturity. How does it happen?

The great divide: those who know God, and those who don't know God.

*God is love. But how can
I be sure? How can I know
what He's really like?*

*Why do I need God, anyway?
I'm really not such a bad
person . . .*

DAY 1

No one was really too surprised when the wedding didn't begin on time. There's something about weddings that makes it easy to start late. Perhaps it's because there are so many people who have to get ready. But the bridesmaids had gathered at the appointed place of meeting. There was the usual flurry of last-minute preparations, interspersed with quick glances at the clock.

"Is the bridegroom here yet?"

"No, not yet. But he'll come."

"I wonder what's keeping him?"

"I can't imagine. Surely he'll be here soon."

But he didn't come. And didn't come. And still didn't come.

The bridesmaids' gowns were spotless. Every hair was in place. Each girl carried a brightly burning lamp and was ready to join the marriage procession. Each was looking eagerly for the bridegroom to arrive so that the ceremony could begin. But still he didn't come.

As minutes passed by, and then hours, the girls grew restless. Then tired. One by one they carefully set their lamps aside and found a comfortable place to sit while they waited. The evening was quiet. The day had been a busy one. At last all ten of the bridesmaids had fallen asleep. And no wonder—it was nearly midnight, and still the bridegroom hadn't come.

At midnight a cry was made. "Here he comes now!"

They were on their feet at once. The flurry of last-minute preparation began anew. To their dismay, they discovered their lamps had burned low. The oil was almost gone, and the flames were ready to go out. Five hurried to refill their lamps, but five had no extra oil. They had not prepared for such a long wait. And even as they watched, their lights flickered and went out.

"Doesn't anyone have extra oil?" The question was repeated, but no one had any extra. The bridegroom appeared. It was time for the procession to begin. The five who had oil in their lamps joined the procession. But the five whose lamps had gone out had hurried away to find a place where they could buy or borrow more oil.

AN OIL SHORTAGE

It was past midnight now, and although the five bridesmaids hunted all over town, there was no oil to be found. Finally they returned to the wedding. "We've missed the procession and the ceremony," they said. "But maybe we can at least get in on the reception."

But when they arrived at the reception hall, they found that the door was shut. Sounds of music and laughter were heard. They knocked, and knocked again. At last the door was opened by the bridegroom himself.

"Let us in," they cried. "We're supposed to be in the wedding."

The bridegroom examined the girls before him. They looked more like street urchins than bridesmaids. Their gowns were rumpled and spotted. He didn't recognize them. Slowly he shook his head. "I don't even know you," he said. And he shut the door. They had missed the wedding.

"I DON'T EVEN KNOW YOU"

Jesus is the one who first told this story about the wedding. You can read it in your Bible, in the twenty-fifth chapter of Matthew. He was trying to impress His hearers with the importance of knowing God for themselves. It was because the bridegroom didn't know the five girls that he would not admit them to the banquet hall.

The same truth is also taught in Matthew 7:21-23. Jesus tells of some who come, in the last day, claiming to be His followers. But they are sent away. The reason is given, "I never knew you."

Knowing God is what Christianity, and religion, and life eternal is all about. The Bible says, "This is life eternal, that they might know thee the only true God, and Jesus Christ, whom thou hast sent" (John 17:3).

But there are conflicting ideas of what God is like. Some say He is vengeful, angry, and arbitrary. Others picture Him as a sort of Santa Claus, whose primary purpose is to fulfill the wishes of His people. Still others say He is like a giant marshmallow, who wouldn't hurt anybody and who is easily swayed and permissive.

We're told that God is love. But we are also told of His anger, His wrath, and His punishments. Insurance companies classify natural disasters as "acts of God." People who suffer often ask the question "Why is God doing this to me?" Preachers talk about God's love, mercy, and patience on the one hand, and about His fiery judgments on the other. And those who listen wonder.

The purpose of this book is to help you discover for yourself what God is really like. It is written to show how you can learn to know Him, whom to know is life eternal. Personal fellowship with God is God's goal for each one of us. He is longing to become our friend. He says to us today, "Yea, I have loved thee with an everlasting love: therefore with lovingkindness have I drawn thee" (Jer. 31:3). He is waiting for us to respond to His love and enter into fellowship with Him. But in order to do this, we must come to know for ourselves what He is really like.

HOW GOD IS REVEALED

One way to get acquainted with God is to look for God revealed in nature. David talked about it in Psalm 19:1: "The heavens declare the glory of God; and the firmament sheweth his handywork." Psalm 77:19 says, "Thy way is in the sea, and thy path in the great waters." In Psalm 104:24 we read, "O Lord, how manifold are thy works! in wisdom thou hast made them all: the earth is full of thy riches."

We can see God in nature. He is portrayed in the glowing sunset, the summer sky, the swallow's effortless flight. We can be reminded of Him as we look upon snow-topped mountains, grassy hillsides covered with flowers, or the unexpected blossoms of the desert. From nature we can learn something of the love of God.

The revelation of God in nature is an important one. God went so far as to set apart one day in seven to remind us of His creative power. You can read it in Exodus 20. The command is given to remember the seventh day, and then the reason for the command is given in verse 11: "For in six days the Lord made heaven and earth, the sea, and all that in them is, and rested the seventh day: wherefore the Lord blessed the sabbath day, and hallowed it."

The things of nature remind us not only of God's love and care for all His creatures but also of the fact that *He* is the *Creator*. We are only creatures. The seventh day was given as a memorial of Creation. The memorial was not initiated after the Fall of man. It was needed to remind us of the nature of man—not merely the *sinful* nature of man, but the *dependent* nature of man, as creature. That is why the special day of worship is not limited to one particular time or nation. God's relationship to His creatures, and His constant care for them, teach of His love.

BUT FLOWERS FADE . . .

Nature, however, has a darker side. The flowers fade. The spotted fawn is dragged down and killed by wolves. Winter snow brings slow starvation to many of the wild creatures. Where is God's love then? Even in the most beautiful and peaceful scenes, if we look again, we can see signs of death and decay. In spite of the evidences still remaining that remind us of the Creator God, there are also evidences everywhere of the effects of sin. Nature can and does represent God—but only imperfectly.

HUMAN LOVE REVEALS GOD'S LOVE

God is revealed through the ties of human love. We can see Him depicted in the mother who cuddles her sleeping baby in her arms. We can see His care in the father carrying his small son on his shoulders. We can see Him in the teacher or pastor who takes the extra time to listen. God's unfailing longing for us is manifest in the weeping mother at the execution of the hardened criminal—still her son. God's love is seen in the companionship and concern of friends and loved ones.

The Bible talks about this revelation of God's love. "Like as a father pitieth his children, so the Lord pitieth them that fear him" (Ps. 103:13). "Can a woman forget her sucking child, that she should not have compassion on the son of her womb?" (Isa. 49:15). "Greater love hath no man than this, that a man lay down his life for his friends" (John 15:13).

But what about the man in Madera, California, who beat his little 6-year-old girl because she wouldn't cry? He beat her for half an hour. And then she said, "Daddy, can I have a drink of water?" And she died. Where was the love of God then? What about the battered babies, the neglected children, the broken homes, broken friendships, broken hearts? How can God's love be revealed in those? Even in Scripture we are reminded of the limitations of human love, in comparison with divine love. Isaiah 49:15 goes on to answer the question "Can a woman forget her sucking child?" by saying, Yes, she may forget. Human love can represent the love of God—but only imperfectly.

THE BIBLE REVEALS GOD

God is revealed in His Word, the Bible. We are told there that He is slow to anger, and of great kindness (Jonah 4:2). We are told that He delights in mercy (Micah 7:18). We are told that God is love (1 John 4:8). But have you ever read the Bible and found yourself in difficulty? Have you ever wondered about the God of the Old Testament? Have you ever pondered the judgments and thunder and threatenings of the God of the Israelites? Even in the Bible it is possible, with our limited understanding, to find ourselves in complete misunderstanding of God, His character, and what He is really like. How easy it is to get a mistaken idea of God if we look only at the surface.

JESUS REVEALS WHAT GOD IS LIKE

Even Jesus' disciples had misunderstandings about what God is like. Yet they wanted to know Him. You can read it in John 14. Philip asked, "Why don't You show us the Father? We'd like to see Him!"

A student said to me one time, "I kind of like Jesus, but I don't like God."

"Why not?"

"Because Jesus is kind, but God is stern, and full of wrath."

Is this a true picture? Is Jesus the one who is loving, and is God stern, harsh, and unforgiving?

How did Jesus answer Philip's request to see God? He said, "Have I been with you all this time and you still don't know Me? If you've seen Me, you've seen the Father. I am in the Father, and He is in Me. The words, the works, that I do are my Father's, for He dwells in Me."

Jesus' mission was to come to a world that was in complete misunderstanding of God, to demonstrate to them what the Father is really like, what He has always been like, and will always be like. The best way to know God is to learn to know Jesus. Jesus' life and death give the clearest picture to be found anywhere of what God is like. He said: "If you know Me, then you know My Father, also" (see John 14:7).

"A CERTAIN MAN HAD A FIG TREE . . ."

In Luke 13 Jesus told a parable to illustrate the character and love of God. Beginning with verse 6: "He spake also this parable; A certain man had a fig tree planted in his vineyard; and he came and sought fruit thereon, and found none. Then said he unto the dresser of his vineyard, Behold, these three years I

come seeking fruit on this fig tree, and find none: cut it down;
why cumbereth it the ground? And he answering said unto him,
Lord, let it alone this year also, till I shall dig about it, and . . .
[fertilize] it: and if it bear fruit, well: and if not, then after that
thou shalt cut it down.''

Who is involved in this dialogue? At first glance it might be
easy to conclude that God, as the owner of the vineyard, is
talking to Jesus, the dresser of the vineyard. And that God says,
''Cut it down.'' But Jesus comes to the rescue and does His best
to calm God down, to get God to have a little mercy.

Not at all. Look again at the parable. If ''God was in Christ,
reconciling the world unto himself'' (2 Cor. 5:19), then God is
equally concerned with our salvation. So what we see in this
story are the two sides of both the Father and the Son, and
probably the Holy Spirit as well. We're seeing the two sides of
God's character—His justice, and His mercy. It isn't Jesus
pleading with God to cool off. It is God, in the three Persons of
the heavenly Family, involved with the balance between justice
and mercy. Justice is an inescapable part of God's character—
and we can be thankful for that, can't we? But mercy is also a
definite part of His character. And we can be thankful for that as
well.

Jesus made it clear when He was here that He came, ''not
. . . to destroy men's lives, but to save them'' (Luke 9:56). And
we read in John 3:16, 17, ''For God so loved the world, that he
gave his only begotten Son, that whosoever believeth in him
should not perish, but have everlasting life. For God sent not his
Son into the world to condemn the world; but that the world
through him might be saved.'' Somehow, in the heart of God,
His mercy is equal to His justice, for we see the cross on a lonely
hill. Even though God's mercy in no way does away with His
justice, because of the cross we see the mingling of the two in the
beautiful plan of salvation. And year after year, century after

century, we continue to hear the words "Let unrepentant sinners alone. Let them alone this year also. Let them alone until I work with them some more, until once again I do my best to win them." And God tries again, and again, and again, to reach us with His love.

BEHOLD THE LOVE OF GOD

John the beloved disciple, when trying to describe the great love of God, finally ran out of words. All he could do was invite us to behold it for ourselves: "Behold, what manner of love the Father hath bestowed upon us" (1 John 3:1).

How do we behold the love of God? By looking at Christ. We behold God's love by becoming acquainted with Jesus, by studying the life of Jesus, by meditating upon the teachings of Jesus. Because Jesus is God. John 1:1, 2 says, "Before anything else existed, there was Christ, with God. He has always been alive, and is himself God" (T.L.B.).

One day in a class I was teaching, we were talking about the love of God. A student raised his hand and asked, "If God loved the world so much, why didn't He come to die Himself? Why did He send His Son?"

Another student, obviously a father, replied, "If you have a son whom you love, it is much *easier* to suffer yourself than to watch your son suffer."

I'm thankful today for a God who loved us enough to send the greatest gift of Himself in His Son to reveal His true character. I'm thankful for Jesus, who was willing to come and give His life a ransom for many. It is good news that the heart of God the Father beats with the same love for us that His Son, Jesus, revealed in His life here on earth. We can rejoice today for the revelation of God's love that is given in nature, in human love, and in the Word of God. And we can also make use of the tremendous opportunity of knowing God that is to be found in a study of the life and teachings of Jesus, where God's love is always most clearly understood.

BUT WHY DO I NEED TO KNOW GOD, ANYWAY?

No one is going to take the time and put forth the effort to come into acquaintance and fellowship with God unless he realizes a need. Jesus said it Himself in Matthew 9:12, 13: "They that be whole need not a physician, but they that are sick. . . . I am not come to call the righteous, but sinners to repentance." No one is really going to thank Jesus for knocking at the door of the heart or open the door to let Him in unless he first realizes his great need for fellowship and communion with Him. No one ever becomes personally acquainted with God unless he first realizes his need for that relationship.

Why do we need God, anyway? It's an important question. We could approach the answer from a secular standpoint, on the basis of logic and reason, as we begin to find an answer.

Several years ago I attended San Francisco State College one summer. Ninety-five percent of the students I associated with there believed that all there was to life was here and now—that's all. It seemed to be the sophisticated thing to believe that we live all our life on this planet, we live out our threescore years and ten, and then we die, and we're dead for a long time—like forever.

Frankly, I wasn't too impressed with their option! It wasn't a matter of making a choice between life forever in heaven or life forever in Las Vegas. It was choosing between life forever in heaven or no life at all! Why, just on the basis of logic and reason, their so-called enlightened belief didn't have much to offer. Let's consider it.

Suppose that you are not a Christian and that I, as a Christian, come to you and give you a fifty-fifty chance that you are right: there is nothing more than the here and now, and when you die, that's it. But you must then give me a fifty-fifty chance that I'm right: that heaven is a real place and that God is a real person. Wouldn't that be playing the game fair? After all, in spite of the fact that I can't prove God or heaven in a test tube, you can't prove that He *doesn't* exist, either. Right? Let's agree that neither one of us can prove our position.

So we start out on an equal footing and shake hands on our agreement. I'll give you a fifty-fifty chance that you're right, if you'll give me a fifty-fifty chance that I'm right.

Let's say that we proceed to live out our lives of threescore years and ten. And when we come to the end, we discover that you were right—there is no forever. We both die, we're both buried in the same ground. And I haven't lost out on a thing.

But suppose that at the end of our threescore years and ten, one day we look up, and there in the east is a small cloud. It gets bigger, and bigger, and it isn't long until the whole sky is filled with heavenly beings. It turns out that there *is* a life beyond this life. God is real, and angels are real, and heaven is real. Jesus has come back again. What now, if you have turned it down? Why, you will have lost just about everything, because what is life here compared with eternity?

KIDDIE KAMPUS CHOICES

I was invited one time to give an address to a class of kindergarten students who were graduating into first grade. That was an ominous honor. They all came marching in, wearing their little homemade gowns and cardboard mortarboards with the tassels hanging down, and I was supposed to try to say something appropriate!

I had decided that I would have to try to involve them in the address or I would never be able to keep their attention, so I had a problem for them to solve. The problem was this: "Let's pretend that in my left hand I have a note for a million dollars, to be payable when you are 21 years old. And in my right hand I have a dollar that you can have right now. Which would you choose?''

I could see the lollipops and ice-cream bars and bubble gum going by in their minds. So I tried to appeal to them, on the basis of their vast education and the fact that they were now graduates, to give careful consideration to this knotty problem. I was afraid what they were going to decide, so I held them off as long as possible. But when I finally asked for their answer, every one of them chose the same thing. The dollar! And I could tell by their pleased expressions that they knew I would be impressed with their careful thinking!

Did that problem end at Kiddie Kampus? No, the whole world is hooked on the same thing. We've been called the Now Generation. And until we realize the need for something beyond just the here and now, we will continue to make the same type of choice as these graduates did.

One day my dad came to me and said, ''Son, I have a proposition to make to you. I want to give you a million dollars.''

And I laughed! I knew a little bit more about my dad's bank account than that!

But he persisted. ''Pretend that I'm a multimillionaire and that I'm going to give you a million dollars. Are you interested?''

''Of course.''

He continued. ''There are two conditions. First of all, you have to agree to spend the whole million in one year.''

Well, I would have preferred to spread the fun out over a longer period of time, but better a million for one year than no million at all.

''The second condition is that at the end of the year, you die in the gas chamber.''

And I said, "I beg your pardon?"

He said, "At the end of the year, you die. There's no way out. You can't use the money to get lost on some tropical island. It is a sure thing that you'll die at the end of the year. Are you still interested?"

I said, "No way!"

"Why not?"

"Because I'd be spending the whole year thinking about the gas chamber. And that would spoil even the fun of one year."

I've tried that out on many people since that time, and the answer is usually the same. It is not that good a deal to trade one year, even if it is a fantastic year, for a whole lifetime.

THE MORAL OF THE STORY!

Then my father came in with the punch line that you could expect a preacher to give his preacher's kid! "Now pretend that I am the devil, and I make you a similar offer. I say, 'You can have seventy years to do exactly as you please. No rules, no regulations. You can do anything, go anywhere. No inhibitions, no morality, no restrictions. Have fun. Live it up. But at the end of the seventy years you will end up in the lake of fire with me.'"

And my dad said, "Are you interested?"

There are thousands of people who have accepted this offer and thought they were making a wise choice.

Most of us are willing to accept the premise that it would be foolish to settle for one year when seventy years are available. But what about settling for seventy years when you could have eternity? It's foolish, even on the basis of logic and reason, to turn down God's offer of eternal life. But thousands have turned it down and will turn it down. Thousands will settle for the temporary pleasures and lose eternity.

THE SCORPION AND THE FROG

A scorpion wanted to cross the river. But he couldn't swim. So he asked a frog to carry him across.

The frog refused. "I know what you'll do," said the frog. "You'll sting me, and I'll sink to the bottom and drown."

"I wouldn't do that," insisted the scorpion. "If I did that, then I would drown the same as you."

So the frog was convinced, and they started out. Sure enough, halfway across the river the scorpion stung the frog.

As they headed for the bottom, the frog asked sadly, "Why did you do that? Now we're both going to die."

And the scorpion said, "I'm sorry, but I couldn't help it. It is my nature."

THE NATURE OF MAN

Because of their nature, people continue to make the foolish choice of turning down eternity in favor of the here and now. Even many brilliant people end up refusing God's offer of life, settling for life here as the total package. We are slaves to our nature, just as the scorpion was. Being born in this world of sin, we are born sinful by nature. And unless the miracle-working power of God intervenes, no amount of logic and reason will cause us to accept God's offer of eternity.

We know that death has come to all mankind since Adam. "Wherefore, as by one man sin entered into the world, and death by sin; and so death passed upon all men, for that all have sinned" (Rom. 5:12). Death is the wages of sin (chap. 6:23). But babies have died before they even had a chance to "sin." Therefore, we know that everyone since Adam is sinful, whether he ever sins or not. We could list numerous texts of Scripture on this, but is it necessary? Death speaks for itself.

There is even more outstanding Bible proof that we are born

sinful. It is the fact that no one can see the kingdom of God unless he is born again (John 3:3). If this is true, then there must be something wrong with our first birth. Well, what is wrong with our first birth? Here we can go back to Augustine, the founder of the classic doctrine of original sin. There's been a lot of debate about Augustine's doctrine. Basically he taught that we are born sinners and held *responsible* for sin from birth. Which means that his doctrine should have been labeled the doctrine of original guilt.

You can have problems with Augustine's doctrine of original guilt, but there is a legitimate Bible doctrine of original sin. It is found in the historic Augsburg Confession, which says that we are born separated from God. That is the real issue. But even though we are born separated from God, we are not held *responsible* for that. Therefore, you don't have to do some ritual to a baby or for a baby in order for him to be saved, because the baby is not held responsible for his birth into this world of sin. No one is held responsible for being born into this world of sin until he has had opportunity to understand the problem intelligently, see his condition, and see what can be done to remedy it. Then his responsibility begins.

That's the Biblical concept of original sin, and I'm thankful for it. John 9 talks about it, John 15 talks about it, James 5 talks about it, and Romans (the first few chapters) talks about it. God has never held us responsible for being born in a world of sin. And that's good news!

BUT OUR HEART IS EVIL AND WE CANNOT CHANGE IT

When we talk of original sin, we are not implying that sin passes from one to another through the genes and chromosomes. There is insufficient evidence to believe that. No, mankind is born separated from God. The practical result of this is that man is born self-centered, and this self-centeredness is the root of all the sins that follow (Rom. 8:7). We are born hopelessly self-centered. And although many people have trouble thinking of a newborn baby as being sinful, few should have problems in realizing that a newborn baby is self-centered!

So we can come up with a twofold definition for *sin*—sin, singular; and sins, plural. Sin, singular, is any life that is apart from God. And sins, plural, are the bad things that are done as a result of living apart from God.

Sin, singular, is living a life apart from God, and it makes no difference how good a life that might be. There are many people who live good, moral lives apart from God. But they are living in sin. Whether or not they ever do anything wrong, they are living in sin. Their good lives are sin. Can you buy that? Romans 14:23 says it: "Whatsoever is not of faith is sin." And anything I do that is not done through the faith relationship with Jesus is sin—even mowing the widow's lawn. Because if I am self-centered from living a life apart from God, then I can mow the widow's lawn only for selfish reasons. It is possible to do all the right things for all the wrong reasons.

What are the selfish motives that can prompt me to mow the widow's lawn? Well, perhaps I'm going on vacation before too long, and I hope she'll feed my dog while I'm away. Perhaps I am hoping the neighbors will see me as I mow the widow's lawn, for this will give me a good reputation among them. Or perhaps I've committed some terrible sin and I'm trying to atone for it. Or maybe I've heard that she's tottering on the edge of life, and I'm hoping she will remember me in her will. There can be all kinds of reasons for mowing the widow's lawn; maybe some of them I wouldn't even be able to identify. But the point is that anyone who is living a life apart from Jesus is going to do whatever right things he does for wrong, self-centered reasons.

It is the sinful *condition* of mankind that results in sinful deeds, whether the deeds are thought of as right or wrong. Man sins because he *is* sinful. He is not sinful because he sins. Notice again that the major issue in sin is separation from God. You don't have to sin to be sinful; all you have to do is get yourself born!

Were we to try to put all this into equation form, we might say that Mankind = Sin, and Righteousness = Jesus. Jesus is the only one born into this world who was not born sinful, not born separated from God. Jesus is the only one who was ever born righteous. It is clear from this analogy that the only possibility for righteousness, as far as man is concerned, would be Mankind + Jesus = Righteousness. Mankind without Jesus is still sinful. The real issue in sin and righteousness is whether or not Jesus is in the life.

We were talking about this in a class one day when a student in the back figuratively whipped out his pocket calculator and said, "Wait a minute! You say that Jesus = Righteousness, all by Himself. Then you say that Mankind + Jesus = Righteousness. If that is true, then Mankind = Nothing!"

And he had the worried look on his face as if I had just done an injustice to the human race! What do we mean when we say that Mankind = Nothing?

HELPLESS, BUT NOT WORTHLESS

Mankind equals nothing as far as *righteousness* is concerned. What does the Bible say? "All our righteousnesses are as filthy rags" (Isa. 64:6). But this does not mean that mankind is worth nothing as far as *worth* is concerned. There is a tremendous difference between being helpless to produce righteousness and being worthless. Our worth was proved when Jesus came to this little world, a mere speck in the universe, to redeem mankind from sin. This tells us of the tremendous value of the human soul.

I once heard it said that if we could take a giant balance and put the whole world, which weighs 6 sextillion tons, on one side of it, and then put a little baby on the other side, the balance would tip in the baby's favor. Such is the worth of the human soul. So we don't have to go around with our heads hanging; we can stand straight and tall, because of the worth put on us by Jesus Christ. But we are still helpless to produce righteousness. Do you see the difference between being helpless and being worthless?

NO INTEREST IN SPIRITUAL THINGS

Not only are we helpless to produce righteousness apart from Christ, but we have a much more major problem that comes from being born separated from God. That is, we have no interest in spiritual things. We find no joy in communion with God. It's actually distasteful to us. One of the greatest evidences that a person has not been born again—is still living apart from God—is the lack of interest in spiritual things.

I had a friend who preached a sermon one day about the man who got to heaven by mistake. Someone came in a little late and didn't hear the whole sermon. This person went away spreading the tale that the preacher was saying that it is possible for people to end up in heaven by mistake. Well, that wasn't his point. He was trying to picture what it would be like for the sinner, who had not been born again, who had no joy in holiness, no joy in communion with God, no joy in unselfish service for others, to find himself in heaven. How miserable such a person would be there! Have you ever considered it an evidence of the love of God that He allows those who refuse salvation not to be in heaven? It would be a place of torture to them. It is only after one has been born again that he finds joy in spiritual things.

MANKIND NEEDS A SAVIOUR

If the real issue in sin is living a life apart from God, then where should our primary focus be? Should we place our effort and attention on the good or bad things we do, or should we place it on the relationship of union and fellowship with the Saviour, the Lord Jesus Christ?

If everyone in the world, except Jesus, is born sinful (Rom. 3:23), then everyone in this world needs a Saviour in order to be saved (Acts 4:12). The gospel is the good news of Jesus (Rom. 1:16). Jesus, our Saviour, provided salvation at the cross, through which the power of sin is broken. When a sinner accepts this great salvation, he is born again, and the greatest trade ever made takes place.

Suppose I were to offer to trade my ball-point pen for a Cadillac Seville. If there were someone with that sort of car who would trade with me, either he would be stupid or he would really love me a lot, one of the two. It would be quite a trade, wouldn't it?

The Bible talks about the greatest trade ever, in 2 Corinthians 5:21: "For he [that is, God] hath made him [that is, Jesus] to be sin for us, who knew no sin; that we might be made the righteousness of God in him." We could change the wording just a bit: For God hath made Jesus, who knew no sin, to be sin for us that we, who knew no righteousness, might be made the righteousness of God in Him.

Would you like to have Jesus, with His wide-open arms and friendly eyes, come to you today and offer to trade all His righteousness for all your sins? Would you be interested? The truth is that this is exactly what He offers to do. And yet, in this greatest trade ever, it would appear at first that someone will end up with the small end of the deal. It's something like trading a Cadillac Seville for a ball-point pen, except there's no ball-point pen! All we have to trade for His righteousness are filthy rags, as Isaiah calls all our righteousness (Isa. 64:6). You can come to only one conclusion—either the One who offers to make this trade is very foolish or else He must really love us a lot.

IT'S NOT WHAT YOU DO, BUT WHOM YOU KNOW

In Ephesians 2:8, 9 we find some significant words: "For by grace are ye saved through faith; and that not of yourselves: it is the gift of God: not of works, lest any man should boast." Paul says repeatedly, as in Romans 3:20, "By the deeds of the law there shall no flesh be justified." In other words, salvation is based not upon what you do, but upon whom you know. And no person really sees the necessity for knowing God—and therefore sees the need to reserve quality time for that purpose—until he realizes that salvation is based upon relationship instead of behavior.

If you are hoping for salvation but see no need for knowing God and do not consider time with God important, then you still believe that your salvation is based upon your behavior. Regardless of what a person says about his beliefs, if he is convinced that salvation and Christianity are based upon a relationship with Christ, then that relationship has to become top priority. Anyone who does not seek for salvation through fellowship with God and through knowing Him on a one-to-one basis is a legalist, trying to gain heaven by his own works.

KNOWING GOD IS THE BOTTOM LINE

When we come to understand that we are sinful by nature and what it is that causes sin in the first place, we can better understand the need for knowing God. Righteousness is never an entity in itself. It comes only with Jesus. When I accept Jesus as my Saviour, my Lord, and my Friend, I have all of His righteousness, because His righteousness comes with Him.

But there is another reason why knowing God is important. It is important for *God's* sake. Think of all the grief and sorrow that has come to *His* heart, through the centuries, because of sinful man's determination to go his own way.

When you really love someone, you want more than anything else for him to love you, too. God really *is* love, and He really does love us a lot, as shown in His offer to exchange all our sin for all His righteousness. It's a fantastic offer for us—but what about for Him? Does He end up being cheated in this greatest of all trades? To answer, I'd like to resurrect an old story that's to the point. It's the story of Old Joe.

Old Joe was a slave down near the mouth of the Mississippi. One day he was on the block at the slave market, the same place where Abraham Lincoln later stood and watched the tears flow and the hearts break and said, "If I ever get a chance to hit that thing, I'll hit it hard!" Joe stood there, sick and tired of separation and tears and partings. He had determined that he would never work again. But he was on the auction block. The bidders began to bid, and Joe began to mutter, under his breath at first and then louder and louder, "I won't work. I won't work." He was heard, and one by one the bidding dropped off, except for one man who traded good money for this slave who wouldn't work.

The new master took Joe to his carriage and drove out into the country to the plantation. Finally he went down a little road that passed a lake. Beside the lake was a beautiful cabin with curtains at the windows and flowers by the cobblestone steps. Joe had never seen anything like it.

"This is where I'm going to live?" Joe asked.

"Yes."

"But I won't work."

"Joe, you don't have to work. I bought you to set you free." (The best part of the story is still to come.)

Joe fell at the feet of his benefactor and said, "Master, I'll serve you forever."

You see a group of sinners. They have been slaves to sin and pain and death. They say, "We won't work—we *can't!*" Have you ever tried it? Have you ever tried to produce the works of righteousness? It's impossible. You can't do it.

But Jesus says, *"You* don't have to work. I've bought you, with My own blood, to set you free, and I want to live My life in you."

I understand He has some mansions by a lake that looks like a sea made out of glass. There are cobblestones and curtains, and flowers that will never fade. He offers us all this because He loves us. That's the way He is. And when we understand this trade and it really gets through to our heart, we will gladly serve Him forever.

*What are the steps in
coming to Christ? How can
I know whether I am saved?*

*How can I become personally
acquainted with a God whom
I can't see or hear?*

DAY 2

He was an old man with thin gray hair, deep wrinkles, and the trembling hands of one who has already used up his threescore years and ten. I met him only once, but I have never forgotten him. It was at an old-fashioned summer camp meeting, in the main tent just after the sermon for the morning had been given. The platform chairman asked for each of the pastors who were present at the meeting to take a section of the congregation and lead out in a short after meeting to give opportunity for the audience to make comments or ask questions. This man was in my section. He stood to his feet and with tears in his eyes said, "For a long time God tried to get me, and He finally got me." And he sat down.

I don't remember what anyone else said that day, but I still remember him. How wonderful, and how tragic. How wonderful that God finally won out in the battle for his life—but how tragic that he had waited so long.

Hannah Whitall Smith tells the story of a man who came to Christ, and in telling his experience she says that it happened after he had finally come to understand what was his part and what was God's part. Well, Christians have often debated what is man's part and what is God's part in coming to Christ and in continuing the Christian life. So the man was immediately asked, "What exactly was your part, and what was God's part?"

He replied, "My part was to run, and God's part was to catch me!"

Jesus said in John 6:44, "No man can come to me, except the Father which hath sent me draw him." Salvation is God's initiative, not man's. Jeremiah 31:3 says, "I have loved thee with an everlasting love: therefore with lovingkindness have I drawn thee." And God's lovingkindness extends to every person. There are not some destined to be saved and others destined to be fuel for the fires of hell. Everyone is drawn by God. And only those who persistently resist His drawing power of love will not come to Him for salvation.

However, in the process of being drawn to Christ there are certain steps that we take in coming to Him. What are these steps? First, there is a desire for something better. Second, there comes a knowledge of what it is that's better. Third comes the conviction that we are sinners. Fourth, we are brought to realize that we are helpless to do anything at all about our condition. And finally, we give up—it's called "surrender" in Christian circles. We give up on ever being able to save ourselves, and then we can come to Christ just as we are.

Let's go over these five steps in greater detail as we try to understand the process that each person goes through in coming to Christ.

DESIRE FOR SOMETHING BETTER

In John 4 is the story of a woman who came to Jesus. Notice the first steps she took in coming to Him.

Begin with verses 5 and 6: "Then cometh he [Jesus] to a city of Samaria, which is called Sychar, near to the parcel of ground that Jacob gave to his son Joseph. Now Jacob's well was there. Jesus therefore, being wearied with his journey, sat thus on the well: and it was about the sixth hour" (or twelve o'clock noon).

Here you have a strange enigma. Jesus is the Creator. He is God. He's the one who made the suns and stars and systems. He created everything that was made (chap. 1:3). And yet He had accepted the burden of humanity and was apparently even more tired than His disciples, for they went on to Sychar to buy food. Being too tired to go farther, He sat alone on the edge of the well and waited for their return. Can you see Him there?

Continue the story with verse 7 of John 4: "There cometh a woman of Samaria to draw water: Jesus saith unto her, Give me to drink."

Here we see the Master at work, drawing a soul to Him. He doesn't try to cram His religion down her throat. Instead, He asks a favor of her. Trust awakens trust.

"Then saith the woman of Samaria unto him, How is it that thou, being a Jew, askest drink of me, which am a woman of Samaria? for the Jews have no dealings with the Samaritans.

"Jesus answered and said unto her, if thou knewest the gift of God, and who it is that saith unto thee, Give me to drink; thou wouldest have asked of him, and he would have given thee living water.

"The woman saith unto him, Sir, thou hast nothing to draw with, and the well is deep: from whence then hast thou that living water? Art thou greater than our father Jacob, which gave us the well, and drank thereof himself, and his children, and his cattle?

"Jesus answered and said unto her, Whosoever drinketh of this water shall thirst again: but whosoever drinketh of the water that I shall give him shall never thirst; but the water that I shall give him shall be in him a well of water springing up into everlasting life.

"The woman saith unto him, Sir, give me this water, that I thirst not, neither come hither to draw.

"Jesus saith unto her, Go, call thy husband, and come hither.

"The woman answered and said, I have no husband.

"Jesus said unto her, Thou hast well said, I have no husband: for thou hast had five husbands; and he whom thou now hast is not thy husband: in that saidst thou truly" (verses 9-18).

Obviously this woman had a desire for something better. She had come to draw water. Apparently she was a harlot from the nearby town, because she came at a time when none of the rest of the women from town came. She also came to a well that was outside of town. She had grown tired of the glances and the gossiping tongues. She had come alone to the well to escape their condemnation.

We know that she was looking for something better that she hadn't found yet. She had been married, but her first husband was not what she was after, so she looked for something better in a second husband. And that wasn't good enough, so she looked for something better in a third husband, and a fourth, and a fifth. And finally she was done with marriage and decided to follow the path that many are following today, to just go ahead and live with someone and not make a commitment that she could not keep. And we see her approaching the well, still looking for something better.

NEVER SATISFIED

A friend of mine told me about a man he knew who started smoking. He smoked Chesterfields, because they were advertised as the cigarette that satisfies. But he wasn't satisfied. He started out with one pack a day, but that wasn't enough, so he tried two packs a day. And that still wasn't enough, so he increased it to three. Never satisfied.

Everyone in this world is looking for something better. Boys and girls are looking for a better bicycle or a better ball. Young people look for more acceptance, better friends, more fun. Older people look for success, for pleasure, or for material possessions. But even things that look like legitimate desires can represent the heart cry of a person who has a God-shaped vacuum in his life that can be filled only by God Himself.

There are mountain climbers who climb mountains because they are there. The rock climbers keep looking for a higher rock, for greater risks. Ambition in sports, in business, in legitimate pleasures, can be the cry of the heart for something better, the unrecognized desire for God.

But the desire for something better is never satisfied apart from God. The person who looks for happiness in the world finds that the fun the world has to offer does not last. And he must always be searching for something new to help him forget that the latest thing he thought would be satisfying didn't last.

As Jesus said in verse 13 of this chapter about the woman of Samaria, "Whoever drinketh of this water shall thirst again." And all our efforts toward finding something better apart from God will end in nothing, because whether we recognize it or not, our desire is for Him.

There are sidetracks at every step of the way to Christ, to prevent us from coming to Him. We try to satisfy our desire for something better by trying something different. You see it in the story of the woman of Samaria. She had tried to satisfy her desire for something better by seeking fulfillment in multiple human relationships. But in spite of the many different things she had tried, her desire remained unsatisfied.

Jesus said, "Whosoever drinketh of this water shall thirst again: but whosoever drinketh of the water that I shall give him shall never thirst." Most of us take the long route to God, the route of trouble, and pain, and broken hearts. And when all the things that we thought we wanted go sour, we finally come to the end of our own resources and we then look up and say, "All right, God. I guess I do need You after all."

But there is a shorter route. Jesus offered it to the woman at the well. It's found in John 12:32: "I, if I be lifted up from the earth, will draw all men unto me." When Jesus is uplifed, we are drawn to Him. This Samaritan woman was in the presence of the One who could satisfy all her longings, but she did not realize it. So Jesus moved on to the second step, a knowledge of what it is that's better.

KNOWLEDGE OF THE PLAN OF SALVATION

Notice John 4:10: "Jesus answered and said unto her, If thou knewest the gift of God, and who it is that saith to thee, Give me to drink; thou wouldest have asked of him, and he would have given thee living water."

Salvation is the gift of God. That is probably one of the greatest bits of knowledge concerning the plan of salvation that we could ever receive. "For God so loved the world, that he *gave* his only begotten Son" (chap. 3:16). "The wages of sin is death; but the *gift* of God is eternal life" (Rom. 6:23). We can't earn it, we can't purchase it, we can never merit it. Salvation is a gift. It has no relationship to what we deserve.

Think of the ways we try to earn what we want. This Samaritan woman might have been a woman of the streets, accustomed to selling herself to make a living, to try to earn something better. The people who were her customers were wanting something better as well and were willing to pay for a synthetic love to try to satisfy their desires. Many people today try to buy love and acceptance through similar methods. Many people today try to buy *God's* love and acceptance and become nothing more than fornicators in the spiritual sense. But Jesus comes along and says that the greatest pleasure, the lasting happiness, is free. He says to us today as He did to the woman by the well, "If thou knewest the *gift* of God . . ." If you only knew.

The sidetrack to this step is to substitute a knowledge about religious things for a personal knowledge of spiritual things and the plan of salvation. When Jesus brought the woman of Samaria to the knowledge of the free gift of salvation and to the knowledge that He knew her heart, she tried to change the subject. She started a discussion about which place was the best place to worship God. Should it be Jerusalem, or Samaria? She was dodging Jesus' home thrust. But He was patient with her, and He is patient with us. Think of all the times we have veered off course when the pressure got too high. But the Holy Spirit does not leave us, and Jesus is still there in the shadows, waiting for us to stop running. The water of life is still being offered freely today.

Sometimes our knowledge of God is limited. The Samaritan woman's was. In verse 25 of John 4 she said, We know that the Messiah is going to come. There are people today who grew up on that knowledge. It's hard to be anywhere in our society today and miss the talk about the second coming of Christ. But it is possible to *hear* about the Second Coming and *see* the signs that it is drawing near and even *believe* that it will one day happen and still not be drinking at the well of the water of life that Christ offers.

We can be thankful, however, for whatever knowledge of God we have. A little knowledge of Him is better than none. Thank God for what we may have picked up as boys and girls concerning the love of God. The Holy Spirit can use whatever knowledge of God we have to guide us to a deeper relationship with the Lord Jesus.

CONVICTION

The third step in coming to Christ is the realization that we are sinners. We come to realize that we *are* sinful whether we have ever done anything wrong or not. Is there anyone who has never done anything wrong? If there is, that person is still sinful, because one doesn't have to sin to be sinful. All one has to do to be a sinner is to be born. As we noticed in Day 1, we are born sinners, and Jesus said that in order even to see the kingdom of God, we must be born again. Therefore, there must have been something wrong with our first birth.

There are many people who hesitate to take this third step. They say, "I'm just as good as the next person. I'm as good as some I know who claim to be Christians." They fall into the trap of comparing themselves among themselves. There are many sidetracks to this step. One is to think that we are not really sinners, that basically we are good people. There are whole denominations today based on the premise that people are basically good and that all that is necessary is to develop the good that is in them.

But the Bible says in Romans 3:10-12 that "there is none righteous, no, not one." One of the steps in coming to Christ is to come to the point where we are willing to admit this, for it is only the sinner who needs a Saviour.

There is nothing that works so effectively to convince a person that he is a sinner than to take a look at Jesus and the cross. One time I saw a man who was eight feet tall. He was built like a football player and was wearing an Arden's Milk Farm shirt. He was walking across a county fairgrounds. When I first saw him off in the distance, he didn't look that tall, maybe about my size. But when I got up close to him, I felt like a dwarf.

When you spiritually see Jesus off in the distance and you're not that close to Him, He may not look too tall—maybe about your height. But when you get closer to Jesus, you will see that He looms up like a mountain peak with its snowcapped top pushing into the blue, and you will feel like a swamp at the base. That's what happened to the apostle Paul. He thought he was pretty good until he got a glimpse of Jesus. You can read about it in Philippians 3. Once he saw Jesus and was brought close to Him, then everything he had before thought was good he now counted as so much garbage. So it is in looking to Jesus that we are drawn to a realization of our condition as sinners.

HELPLESSNESS

The fourth step is the hardest one yet, because there is something in the human heart that resists admitting that we are helpless. I have occasionally asked students of mine, when we were studying these steps to Christ, to fill out anonymously a questionnaire indicating where on the steps to Christ they found themselves at that time. The majority always placed themselves right here—they realized that they were sinners, but they hadn't yet admitted being helpless to do anything about it themselves.

The sidetrack that many people take at this point is to think that if they try harder or longer, they can make themselves better. But Jesus said in John 15:5, "Without me ye can do nothing." Jeremiah asks the question "Can the Ethiopian change his skin, or the leopard his spots? then may ye also do good, that are accustomed to do evil'' (Jer. 13:23).

After a meeting in Seattle on the subject of our helplessness, I was talking to a doctor. He said to me, ''Your message will never sell! I was at the top of my class in college. I was in the top third of my class in medicine. I have a nice family. I have a house in the city and a mountain cabin. I have a yacht in the harbor and two Cadillacs in the garage. Don't tell me that I'm helpless.''

He had forgotten who it was who was keeping his heart beating, hadn't he? But that isn't the point. There are many people who, like this doctor, can experience worldly success apart from God as long as He keeps their hearts beating. But the point is that we are helpless to produce anything apart from God when it comes to genuine goodness or righteousness. It isn't until a person comes to the realization that he can do nothing to save himself spiritually, and that he can do nothing to keep himself from his present sinning and mistakes and failures, that he is ready to take the next step in coming to Christ. No one ever comes to Jesus until he has admitted failure and realized his helplessness to save himself.

SURRENDER

The word *surrender* means ''giving up.'' What do we give up? We give up on *us!* We give up on the idea that we can do anything at all about our condition, except one—come to Christ just as we are. And Christ loves to have us come to Him just as we are. In fact, that's the only way we can come. We can never become better through our own efforts. We must come just as we are.

The detour that many people take on this step is to try to give up *things* instead of *self*. We try to give up our smoking and drinking and gambling. We have the idea that the Christian life is based on how many things one can give up. If surrender means to give up the idea that we can do anything at all apart from Christ, then for the strong person the giving up of things can become a sidetrack for giving up self.

The story is told about a man whose car horn wouldn't work. So he took the car to the garage to get the horn repaired. It was raining, and when he drove up to the entrance to the garage, he saw that the door was closed. On the door was a sign, "Honk for service." We have often found ourselves in the same dilemma in trying to surrender ourselves. An important truth about surrender is that it is not something *we* can do! This can represent a major breakthrough to the person who has been vainly trying to surrender. The word *surrender* means "to give up." And if coming to the end of our own resources is necessary in order for us to come to Christ, then that helplessness would have to include the helplessness to surrender, too! If I had the strength or ability within myself to surrender, then I wouldn't have to give up on myself—there would still be something I could do.

But surrender is not something we do, even though we do it! What's the point? That only God can lead us to surrender. We cannot bring ourselves there, even though when the time comes, we are the ones who surrender. But no man can empty himself of self. It is only Christ who can do the work. Our part is to consent, and as we proceed we will study more of how it is that we consent.

If you want to kill yourself, there are a number of ways you can do it. You can take a gun and blow your brains out. You can jump off a tall building or bridge. You can take an overdose of some lethal drug. But there is one way in which you can never kill yourself. You cannot crucify yourself. There is no way you can do it. If you are to be crucified, someone else must do the job for you.

The cross is used in Scripture as a symbol of surrender, death to self. Jesus spoke of our cross. He invites us to take up our cross and follow Him (Matt. 16:24). He uses the cross, the crucifixion, as a symbol to teach us that we cannot surrender ourselves; we must allow God to do the work for us. And He is willing and able to bring us to the point of surrender if we will allow Him to do so.

GOD TAKES THE INITIATIVE

A desire for something better comes from God. It is His drawing power that awakens our desire for something more than we have. A conviction that we are sinners is the work of the Holy Spirit: "He will reprove [convict] the world of sin" (John 16:8). A realization of our helplessness is His work, for Jesus said, "Without me ye can do nothing" (chap. 15:5). Bringing us to the point of surrender is His work, even though we are the ones who surrender. There is only one of the five steps in which we can deliberately participate, and that is in gaining the knowledge of the plan of salvation. Although Jesus takes the initiative there as well, we can respond to His initiative by choosing to seek Him, to seek a knowledge of Him. That is the way you consent—by placing yourself in the atmosphere where Jesus works. Whether it is in church, in public meetings, or in private before God's open Word, or perhaps in reading this book, if you will make the one attempt to respond to the drawing of Jesus and His Spirit, to gain a better knowledge of the plan of salvation, He will do the rest.

Jesus still offers today to accept anyone who comes to Him. The invitation is still out, "Come unto me, all ye that labour and are heavy laden, and I will give you rest" (Matt. 11:28). Regardless of where you are, and who you are, and what your past has been, Jesus offers peace to you. If you have never before come to Christ you can come to Him right now.

STEPS TO CHRIST

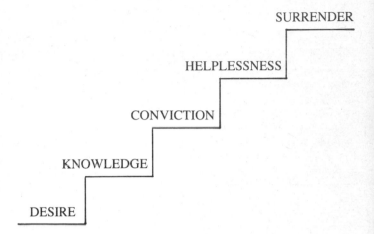

Perhaps you have seen which of the steps to Christ you are on. Do you realize a desire for something better? Do you realize that God is love and that Jesus died for you? Do you realize that you are a sinner? Do you realize that you are helpless to do anything about it? And have you come to the point of giving up on ever being able to do anything about it? Then you can come to Jesus, just as you are, because those are the steps to Him. God is drawing you to Him, and you can respond, and continue to come to Him tomorrow morning and the next, until Jesus Himself comes again.

CONVERSION—THE NEW BIRTH

Once a person has taken these steps to Christ, including surrender to Him, he is born again, or converted. What is conversion? It must be an important step, for Jesus said we can't even see the kingdom of God unless we are born again (John 3:5). Another way to say it would be that unless you are born again, you can't even understand God's grace in its fullness, or really comprehend what the cross and salvation are all about. The new birth is essential before a person can find meaning in the relationship of knowing God. Because knowing God is the entire basis of the Christian life, if a person hasn't been born yet, he's going to have a pretty difficult time trying to live!

Conversion is the supernatural work of the Holy Spirit on the human heart. You'll find that in John 3. It produces a change of attitude toward God. Instead of running from Him, now I'm coming to Him. It creates a new capacity for knowing God that wasn't even there before. That's what makes Bible study and prayer meaningful for the first time. I believe that no one really begins a meaningful relationship with God until he comes to the point of conversion; anyone who tries to have a meaningful fellowship with Him before that point will find one of two things will happen. Either he will be led to conversion or he will become frustrated and scrap the whole thing. One of the two. And the thing that makes the difference is the sense of need. It is only the one who realizes his deep need who will be willing to come to Christ and give up on himself and his own efforts to gain salvation.

Conversion is the beginning of a new life. It is a change of direction. It is *not* a complete and immediate change of behavior. The new birth *leads to* a change in the life style. But it is likened to birth in that it is the beginning of growth. We are not born mature Christians spiritually any more than we are born mature people physically. There is a process. It takes time to develop the fruits of the Spirit in the life—love, joy, peace, long-suffering, and so forth—as listed in Galatians 5. But it is the beginning. And as we continue to seek the relationship with

God, our trust in Him will grow, and we will be changed into His image by beholding Him.

"HOW CAN I KNOW WHETHER I HAVE BEEN BORN AGAIN?"

The question is often asked, "How can I know whether I have been born again?" Here are seven points that may help to answer that question.

1. For the person who has been born again, Jesus is the center and focus of his life. First John 5:12: "He that hath the Son hath life; and he that hath not the Son of God hath not life." What does it mean to have the Son? Well, what does it mean to have a friend or have a husband or a wife? It means simply to have a relationship with him or her. The people in the early Christian church who had experienced a personal relationship with the Son of God couldn't keep quiet about it. They loved to think of Jesus, to talk of Him. And finally the people said, "Let's call them Christians, because Christ is all they talk about."

2. A person who has been born again has a deep interest in Bible study. In 1 Peter 2:2 the apostle Peter describes it as hungering for "the sincere milk of the word." Bible study is meaningful for the converted Christian.

3. One who has been born again is going to find meaning in his prayer life. He may not feel that he is praying properly or effectively, but he is still going to find meaning in talking to God as a vital part of the relationship of knowing God (see John 17:3).

4. A person who has been born again is going to seek a daily experience with Christ. Luke 9:23: "If any man will come after me, let him deny himself, and take up his cross daily, and follow me."

5. A person who has been born again will admit that he is a

sinner. He doesn't go around boasting that he is no longer a
sinner. Paul, one of the greatest Christians who ever lived, said,
"I am the chief of sinners" (see 1 Tim. 1:15). Did this mean that
Paul was sinning all the time? No, because he spoke a number of
times about being more than conqueror through Christ (Rom.
8:37). But he was talking about the fact that apart from God we
are sinful by nature and that only by the grace of God can we
experience anything else. I'm thankful that it is possible to be a
saved sinner. But it's important to realize that we will continue
to be sinful by nature until Jesus comes again (see 1 John 1:8).

6. One of the first symptoms of the new birth is peace
within. Romans 5:1: "Therefore being justified by faith, we
have peace with God." It is possible to have all sorts of external
struggle and trouble and turmoil and still have peace within.
Have you discovered that yet? This inward peace is one of the
first of the fruits of the Spirit—love, joy, peace.

7. And finally, a person who has been born again is going to
have a *desire* to tell someone else what a wonderful friend he has
found in Jesus. Jesus told the demoniac whom He had healed to
go home and tell his friends what great things the Lord had done
for him (Mark 5:19). The desire is there to tell someone else the
good news, although it is possible for the converted Christian to
refuse to share the love of Christ with others (which results in
losing the desire to share). We'll talk more about this in Day 3.

ASSURANCE OF SALVATION

What is the basis of salvation? Let's turn to Ephesians 2:8, 9:
"For by grace are ye saved through faith; and that not of
yourselves: it is the gift of God: not of works, lest any man
should boast." I would like to remind you that nowhere in
Scripture are we told that salvation comes through grace alone.
It is always by grace *through faith*. If that were not true, then
everyone in the world would be saved, and we know that will

never happen. Jesus said, "Enter ye in at the strait gate: for wide is the gate, and broad is the way, that leadeth to destruction, and many there be which go in thereat: because strait is the gate, and narrow is the way, which leadeth unto life, and few there be that find it" (Matt. 7:13, 14). So although God's grace is sufficient for every person, it is no good for anybody until he accepts it. And we accept it by faith.

When you use the word *faith,* you are introducing a relationship element. Even though grace is the gift of God, it must be received by us. And no one can be saved until he accepts the gift that God has provided. Faith demands relationship, one party trusting another. It is possible to accept someone today and reject him tomorrow. It is possible to be married today and not be married ten years from now. In the same way it is possible to accept God's grace at one point and reject it at another. In order to have the continuing assurance of salvation, we must accept God's grace on a continuing basis (chap. 24:13).

This brings us to one of the major texts that tells how we can be assured of eternal life. John 17:3: "This is life eternal, that they might know thee the only true God, and Jesus Christ, whom thou hast sent." There is something more to salvation than to accept God once. And that is to continue to accept Him, today, tomorrow, next week, and every day until He comes again. So eternal life, including our hope of eternal life, is based totally on God's grace, but His grace must be accepted on a continuing basis. And that is what knowing God is all about.

So when we have taken the steps in coming to Christ, have come to the end of our own resources and have accepted Christ as a personal Saviour, we are born again. If I continue in the relationship that began when I came to Christ, my eternal destiny is certain. But if I do not know God as my personal Saviour day by day and accept His grace on a daily basis, then the relationship with Him comes into jeopardy, just as my relationship with a friend or husband or wife breaks down if there is no communication.

Would you like to have the assurance of salvation today? It is offered to every person who comes to Christ and continues coming to Him. The one question you need to ask yourself is this: Do I know Him? Do I spend time in communicating with Him day by day, through His Word and through prayer? Am I on speaking terms with God? For all who continue to seek that faith relationship with Him, eternal life is assured.

THE SPIRITUAL PRESCRIPTION

I used to think that the way to be a Christian was to try hard to live a good life, and that if I had any time left over to read the Bible and pray a little bit, it would make God feel good! It wasn't until much later I discovered that the relationship with God is the entire basis of the Christian life. That's where it's all at. It is not an option. It is not something that we can choose to take or leave. It is the entire basis of the Christian life. And not until I realize and accept that premise am I going to do everything in my power, by God's grace, to find a meaningful communication with God.

There is going to be no such thing as your having a relationship with God and your knowing God unless you spend time together. It's just that simple. My dad used to tell the story of the man who trained his horse not to eat. It was more economical that way. But just when he got him trained, the horse died. And of course, this was the logical conclusion. I might be able to go along living on the "camel's hump" for a period of time, but if I do not eat physically, sooner or later I'll end up in a little heap on the sidewalk, and that will be the end of it. And the person who has experienced the joy of coming to Christ and who has become a Christian may be able to go for a little while without taking time to feed his soul, but sooner or later he's going to end up spiritually in a pitiful little heap on the sidewalk.

When you study the life of Jesus, you find that often He was in communion with His Father. The early morning or the evening hours would be spent in prayer, that He might gain power for His work. If it was necessary for Christ, how much more necessary it must be for us to spend time with God.

When God created this world, even before the entrance of sin, He set aside one day in seven for a time of special communion with His people. There is a rich spiritual blessing for those who will put aside their other activities and spend this time in becoming better acquainted with their Friend and Creator. But in John 6 Jesus makes the analogy between the physical and the spiritual life. Just as it is insufficient to eat only once a week, no matter how nourishing that one meal might be, in the same way we cannot expect to be healthy spiritually by eating spiritual food only once a week.

I'd like to give you a spiritual prescription—a prescription for the vibrant spiritual life. It goes like this: "Take time, alone, at the beginning of every day, to seek Jesus through Bible study and prayer." Let's back up and take a longer look at each of these points.

TAKE TIME

We have learned that salvation comes by grace through faith. What is faith? Faith is trusting God. Faith is trusting someone else. Think for just a moment how you learn to trust someone in this world. In order to trust someone, you must have two things. First, you must have someone who is trustworthy. And second, you must get acquainted with him. And then you will trust him spontaneously. On the other hand, if you have someone who is untrustworthy and you get to know him, you will distrust him spontaneously!

But the premise of the Christian gospel is that God is absolutely trustworthy. Therefore, all you have to do to learn to trust Him is to get to know Him. So how do you get to know Him?

Well, how do you get to know anyone? In order to know someone, you have to communicate with him. And in order to communicate with someone, you have to take time. It is taking time for communication with Him that brings trust. So if we would "fight the good fight of faith" (1 Tim. 6:12), we would be putting forth the effort to become personally acquainted with the One who is trustworthy. It is impossible for a relationship with anyone to grow without setting aside time for communication.

Time. I'd like to propose to you that this is where *all* the deliberate effort in the Christian life must be centered. All of it. I don't spend part of my time and effort on trying to be good and part of it on the relationship with God. I put all my deliberate effort toward spending time with God, and through the experience of faith and dependence upon Him He does the rest of the work of salvation in me.

How much time? Well, reading a Bible text for the day with your hand on the doorknob is not going to suffice. From Jesus' analogy between our physical eating and our spiritual eating, we can learn that we ought to spend at least as much time feeding our spiritual lives as we do feeding our physical lives. And that thoughtful hour or half-hour with God is the most important time of our day.

"Oh, I don't have time," you say. If I don't have time for God, then I don't have time to live. Do you believe that? You know that television has proved to the American public that time is no problem. It has proved again in a modern way the old adage that you have time for what you really consider to be important. So *take time* for knowing God.

TAKE TIME, ALONE

You may have heard the story of the man who was constantly worrying. His friends became concerned; they feared he would go to an early grave because of this. They began worrying about his worrying!

But one day a friend met him on the street and noticed a completely different expression on his face. He was calm and peaceful. And his friend asked, "What's happened? You look so different!"

He said, "I finally found a solution to my worrying."

"Wonderful! What is it?"

He said, "I've hired someone to do my worrying for me."

His friend said, "I never heard of such a thing. How much do you pay him?"

"Four hundred dollars a month."

"Four hundred dollars a month!" the friend exclaimed. "Why, that's impossible! How will you ever be able to pay him?"

"I don't know," he replied. "That's the first thing he has to worry about."

It would be ridiculous to suppose that you could hire someone else to do your worrying for you. It would be ridiculous to suppose you could hire another to do your eating for you. And yet in the spiritual realm it has often been the accepted practice for people to depend upon someone else to do their studying, their praying, and their seeking after God for them.

The Bible teaches that each person must seek God for himself. Let's look first of all at John 1:43-45: "The day following Jesus would go forth into Galilee, and findeth Philip, and saith unto him, Follow me. Now Philip was of Bethsaida, the city of Andrew and Peter. Philip findeth Nathanael, and saith unto him, We have found him, of whom Moses in the law, and the prophets, did write, Jesus of Nazareth, the son of Joseph." Now, right here Philip was showing a bit of immaturity or lack of insight, wasn't he? He should have said, "Jesus from heaven, the Son of God." But "Nathanael said unto him, Can there any good thing come out of Nazareth? Philip said unto him, Come and see" (verse 46). There's the phrase—"Come and see." Whatever mistakes Philip had made earlier he made up for here. You can never miss if you *come and see* for yourself.

Nathanael did come and see for himself, and became a loyal follower of the Lord Jesus.

Earlier in this chapter we studied the story of the Samaritan woman who met Jesus at the well. John 4:28-30: "The woman then left her waterpot, and went her way into the city, and saith to the men, Come, see a man, which told me all things that ever I did: is not this the Christ? Then they went out of the city, and came unto him." Go on to verse 39: "And many of the Samaritans of that city believed on him for the saying of the woman, which testified, He told me all that ever I did." People have often been impressed by the sensational and the spectacular. So, many of them believed because of what she said. And from what we know of this woman, she probably wasn't the most credible person in town. But some of the people believed for a better reason. Notice the rest of the story. "So when the Samaritans were come unto him, they besought him that he would tarry with them: and he abode there two days. And many more believed because of his own word; and said unto the woman, Now we believe, not because of thy saying: for we have heard him ourselves, and know that this is indeed the Christ, the Saviour of the world" (verses 40-42).

In Acts 17:11 it is recorded that the people in Berea were more noble than the ones in Thessalonica because they studied the Word to find out for themselves "whether those things were so." And Paul said to Timothy, in 2 Timothy 2:15, "Study to shew thyself approved unto God, a workman that needeth not to be ashamed." We are to take seriously our relationship with God.

Time *alone*. We must study God's Word for ourselves and pray for ourselves. Only then will family worship and public worship become meaningful. Apart from the private devotional life of each individual, public worship is simply a form or routine. It is when we are on a one-to-one basis with God that we come to know Him for ourselves.

AT THE BEGINNING . . .

Psalm 5:1-3 says: "Give ear to my words, O Lord, consider my meditation. Hearken unto the voice of my cry, my King, and my God: for unto thee will I pray. My voice shalt thou hear in the morning, O Lord; in the morning will I direct my prayer unto thee, and will look up."

Another classic text on the subject is Isaiah 50:4: "The Lord God hath given me the tongue of the learned, that I should know how to speak a word in season to him that is weary: he wakeneth morning by morning, he wakeneth mine ear to hear as the learned." A number of passages in Isaiah, including this verse, have to do with Jesus. And the example of Jesus praying is recorded again and again, as in Mark 1:35: "In the morning, rising up a great while before day, he went out, and departed into a solitary place, and there prayed." Daniel prayed three times a day, morning, noon, and evening (Dan. 6:10). We are invited to follow the examples recorded for our benefit (see 2 Tim. 3:16).

If I am going to be in touch with God and be sensitive to His guidance and depend upon His power instead of my own, and if this is a daily matter, then isn't it kind of late to get my direction for the day just before going to bed at night? If religion is a daily matter, then it's quite obvious when we need the power. It is ridiculous to write a check when you don't have the money in the bank. Hebrews 4 says that Jesus is a faithful High Priest, who "was in all points tempted like as we are" (verse 15). Then it says, "Let us therefore come boldly unto the throne of grace, that we may obtain mercy, *and* find grace to help in time of need" (verse 16). Notice the sequence. During our time with God in the morning we receive power from Him, so that when we draw on that during the day, there will be something there to back our need up.

Some who have trouble in their devotional life and who have been relying upon time spent the last thing before going to bed may find that one of the greatest helps is to change that time to the first thing in the morning. If we take up our cross daily, it makes the most sense to do so when the day begins.

. . . OF EVERY DAY

One of the significant reasons for beginning with God first thing in the morning is for the purpose of consistency. The universal testimony that I have come up against again and again is that when the time alone with God is left for the last thing at night, it becomes spasmodic—on-again, off-again.

The purpose of the daily relationship with Christ is communication. There is no need to ask the question "What happens if I miss a day?" That's not the issue. The important thing is your pattern. If you maintain regular communication, you will have a relationship. It's true with other people, and it's true with God. And if your communication is only sporadic, the relationship will suffer. It is possible even in one day to find yourself at a distance from Jesus, and it may take time to regain the peace that you have lost. Is this because God likes to play hide-and-seek or perhaps punish you for one day's neglect? No. But when we neglect personal communion with God, then there is an enemy who makes the most of it; isn't that true?

The devil will use every maneuver he can to separate us from Jesus and keep us at a distance from Him. We'll look more at some of his methods in Day 3. But when we neglect personal communion with God, Satan does everything possible to keep the separation going. Our only safety lies in determining to give God first priority each day, regardless of what happens. And as we seek Him each day, our friendship and fellowship with Him will deepen.

We are not saved by our devotional life. We are saved by our acceptance of Christ's sacrifice for us at the cross and by continuing to accept Him on a daily basis. But because so many Christians allow the relationship with Christ to disappear, their assurance also disappears. Jesus is often little known even among His professed followers. Little wonder, then, that they find it hard to trust Him for salvation. But when we spend time each day considering and meditating upon His love, how much easier to keep His love fresh in our minds and to believe in His loving acceptance.

TO SEEK JESUS

John the Beloved walked with Jesus for three years. He knew what it was like to eat with Him, to travel with Him, to touch Him, to help Him with His daily needs. And for three years John bickered and argued with the other disciples about who was to be the greatest. For three years he was still the son of thunder. Those who think that conversion and walking with Jesus is supposed to change one completely overnight (and if it doesn't happen, then he doesn't have the genuine experience) had better take a second look at John and Peter and the other disciples. Even in the upper room the night before the crucifixion, they were still scrapping about who was to be the greatest. They knew it was wrong, but they kept doing it, even though they were embarrassed by it. But Jesus treated them kindly, patiently, and even after He had gone back to heaven John and the others continued to walk with Him.

Years later John writes, in his first general Epistle, "That which was from the beginning, which we have heard, which we have seen with our eyes, which we have looked upon, and our hands have handled, of the Word of life; . . . that which we have seen and heard declare we unto you, that ye also may have fellowship with us: and truly our fellowship is with the Father, and with his Son Jesus Christ" (chap. 1:1-3). John says, years after Jesus had returned to heaven, "We have fellowship with Jesus Christ." You can have fellowship with Christ as well. The purpose of the devotional life is to come into fellowship with Jesus Christ. The purpose of walking and talking and communing with Him is for fellowship.

In all our devotional experience the invitation is, the challenge is, to read for the purpose of communication, of fellowship, with Jesus. "We would see Jesus" (John 12:21). Now if we accept that as truth, then this is going to have some influence on what we read.

Not long ago I was reading the book of Joshua. I like to read a little bit out of the Old Testament, along with the New. In the first part of Joshua I read about a lot of battles and victories and the conquering of the peoples of Canaan. In the last half of Joshua I read about meticulous boundaries. It describes the territories of each tribe, how the borders for the tribe of Benjamin went from here and around through here and down to there, and included this and that. After reading a couple of chapters of that, I found it rather hard to see Jesus.

There is a time and purpose for studying each book of the Bible, but if the primary purpose of the devotional life is to seek Jesus, where will I spend most of my time? Studying the last half of the book of Joshua, or studying the Sermon on the Mount? It is possible for the Ten Commandments to become nothing more than a lethal weapon in the hands of one who doesn't know how to sit with Mary at the feet of Jesus and learn of His love and kindness. The law and the gospel must go together. It is as we seek *Jesus* where He is most clearly revealed that we find fellowship with Him and grow more and more into His likeness. The purpose of the devotional life is to learn to know Him and trust Him more fully.

THROUGH BIBLE STUDY . . .

How do you study the Bible for a meaningful devotional life? Again let's underscore the fact that you are looking primarily for Jesus. Eternal life doesn't come from just searching the Scriptures. Read it in John 5:39, 40. The religious leaders did plenty of searching the Scriptures. But they still rejected Jesus and refused to come to Him. It is in coming to Jesus that we have life; the Scriptures are primarily a means to enable us to come to Him.

There was a man of the Pharisees, Nicodemus by name, who came to Jesus by night. He essentially said to Jesus, "You're a great teacher, and I'm not so bad myself. I'm from the Sanhedrin, You know. Let's have a discussion."

Jesus said, "What you need is to be born again." You can read it in the third chapter of John. Nicodemus couldn't understand the things of the kingdom of God, because he had not yet been converted. 1 Corinthians 2:14 says, "The natural man receiveth not the things of the Spirit of God: for they are foolishness unto him: neither can he know them, because they are spiritually discerned."

The understanding of Scripture depends not so much upon the strength of intellect brought to the search as upon the earnest longing after righteousness. The carnal man is at enmity against God. When we have not yet been born again, we will invariably use God's Word for information only. It is when we have been born again that we are enabled for the first time to experience fellowship with Christ through the Scriptures. And the primary purpose of Bible study is not for information, but for communication.

The Bible is not primarily designed as a history lesson. As you read, put yourself in the picture. If you are reading about the woman at the well, *you* are the woman at the well. You are the one who has been seeking to satisfy your heart desire by the things of the world. You are the one who is looking for something better. And you are the one who finally comes face to face with Christ Himself. If you are reading about the lost sheep, *you* are the lost sheep. You are the one that the Shepherd has come searching to find. You are the one who is borne on His shoulders back to the safety of the fold. When you read about the thief on the cross, *you* are the thief on the cross. You are the one who says, " 'Jesus, remember me' " (Luke 23:42, T.L.B.). And you are the one to whom the reply is given, " 'You will be with me in Paradise' " (verse 43, T.L.B.).

Sometimes people ask, "What should I do if my mind wanders?" Well, let me ask you a question. When you were in school and studying for the most boring class you had to take, what did you do when your mind wandered? Did you throw the textbook into the wastebasket and quit school? Or did you keep going back and rereading until you got what you needed to understand?

If the lessons in school have to do with only threescore years and ten, and if the Scriptures have to do with the things of eternity, then shouldn't you at least give the Bible equal running with the schoolbooks?

The primary purpose of Bible study is to enter into communion and fellowship with Jesus. As you invite His presence when you open His Word and seek to put yourself in the picture, to understand what He is saying to you day by day, you will come to know Him better and to trust Him more.

. . . AND PRAYER

Prayer is what makes the Christian church something other than a club or fraternity or secular organization. Prayer makes the difference between Christianity and the other world religions. Without prayer we have nothing more than a Book of information, a creed to try to live by. But the fact that we can actually talk to God, communicate with Jesus Christ, makes prayer a top priority in the Christian life.

Let's turn to Luke 18:10-14 in order to get a setting for the subject of prayer and its significance: ''Two men went up into the temple to pray; the one a Pharisee, and the other a publican. The Pharisee stood and prayed thus with himself, God, I thank thee, that I am not as other men are, extortioners, unjust, adulterers, or even as this publican. I fast twice in the week, I give tithes of all that I possess. And the publican, standing afar off, would not lift up so much as his eyes unto heaven, but smote upon his breast, saying, God be merciful to me a sinner. I tell you, this man went down to his house justified rather than the other: for every one that exalteth himself shall be abased; and he that humbleth himself shall be exalted.''

One of the first prerequisites for a meaningful prayer life is humility. Only the person who has taken the steps to Christ, who has been convinced that he is a sinner and that he is helpless to save himself, is humble and surrendered to Christ. Would it be possible for a person never to understand the deeper meaning of prayer because that person has never come to Christ yet? It is very possible.

But once we understand that the entire basis of the Christian life is the relationship with Christ, and we come to Him for salvation, we will be enabled to pray aright. It was when the publican admitted his sinful condition and came to God, asking for His mercy, that he was justified.

One of the usual ideas of prayer is that its primary purpose is to get answers. I would like to take the position that if your primary purpose in praying is to get answers, it won't be long until you will stop praying. To have life eternal is to be involved in knowing God. And the primary purpose of prayer is to know God. It is primarily for relationship, for communication—not to get answers.

How long would your human relationships last if your only purpose in talking to others was to get answers, to get them to do things for you? Why, we talk to our friends just for the sake of maintaining friendship. And the same thing goes for prayer. Jesus said it in Matthew 6:33: "Seek ye first the kingdom of God, and his righteousness; and all these things shall be added unto you." And it is talking about the necessities of life. God knows our needs. Prayer is not primarily to detail to Him our needs. It is to develop and maintain the friendship with Him.

The subject of prayer is an exhaustless theme. Whole books have been written on the subject and have only scratched the surface. But there is one other point I would like to touch on briefly now, and that is the fact that we should slow down. Many, even in their seasons of devotion, fail to receive the blessing of real communion with God. They are in too great haste. With hurried steps they press through the circle of Christ's loving presence, perhaps pausing for a moment within its sacred precincts but not waiting for counsel. They have no time to remain with the Divine Teacher. With their burdens they return to their work. These can never attain the highest success until they learn the secret of strength. They must give themselves time to think, to pray, to wait upon God for a renewal of physical, mental, and spiritual power. Not a pause for a moment in His presence, but personal contact with Him—this is our need.

Slowing down in your prayer life is one of the greatest secrets to finding personal communion with Christ.

THE DEVOTIONAL LIFE

I'd like to conclude with a brief review of the typical devotional life as outlined in this spiritual prescription.

At the beginning of your day, whatever time that may be according to your occupation, you find some place where you can be alone. First of all, you offer a short prayer for the guidance of the Holy Spirit, that you will be directed in your relationship with God. Then you study something about the life of Christ, focusing on Jesus, and place yourself in the picture with Him. You find yourself taking the steps to Him again for that day, convinced that you are a sinner, realizing you are helpless to save yourself, and giving up yourself to His control.

After you have pondered the passage for that day, you pray a longer prayer, telling God about what you have read. This gives a freshness to each day's prayer life and keeps it from becoming routine, simply repeating certain set phrases.

After talking to God about what you have read, you add whatever petitions you feel inclined to bring, both for yourself and for others. When you've finished your speech, you slow down and wait. You continue in the attitude of prayer, waiting to see whether God wants to communicate something back to you.

I believe that God speaks to us through our mind. At times you will be aware of it, at other times not. But if you stay on your knees and allow God to impress your mind, you will discover that at times He has special messages for you, insights into spiritual truth, or convictions of His plans for you for the day.

WHAT IF IT DOESN'T WORK?

I've often heard people say, "I tried the devotional life, and it doesn't work."

And I've asked, "How long did you try it?"

"Three days."

Why, we don't expect our human relationships to grow that fast! How can we expect our friendship with God to mature in such a short time? So the only conclusion you can come to is that if you determine that from now on you will spend a quiet time alone with God day by day, and if you will continue to do this until Jesus comes again, you will be in fellowship and communion with Him, and you will come to know Him, whom to know is life eternal.

Do you want to know God? Take time, alone, at the beginning of each day, to seek Jesus through His Word and through prayer. And you will become acquainted with the best Friend you'll ever know.

*Will the relationship with
God go sour if I miss a day
or two of communication?*

*How can I still have faith
in Him when everything is
going wrong at once?*

DAY 3

Once upon a time (which should give you a clue as to what sort of story this is going to be) there were two people who loved each other and decided to be married. The husband thought his bride was quite the most beautiful and gentle creature he had ever seen, and the wife thought her new husband was the most fascinating and handsome man in the whole world. The marriage began, as many marriages do, with high hopes and great expectations.

Every morning when the husband had to leave for work he would linger over the goodbyes, and his wife would stand in the doorway and wave, watch the car back out of the drive, and wave again. She didn't go back inside until all that was to be seen was an empty spot down at the corner where the car had turned and gone out of sight. In the evening she would peek out the window every minute or two and would be at the door to welcome him home.

After a while when the husband had to leave for work, he would just gulp down a hot drink and rush out the door. And sometimes she wasn't even out of bed yet. When he came home at night, often he would find her busy at some household task, and she would look up in surprise and say, "Oh, are you home already? I'll be finished here in a few minutes and then I'll start supper." The marriage wasn't over, but the honeymoon was.

Well, one day not too long after this the bride, who was now just a wife, was busy sewing. Somewhere in the back of her mind she expected to be interrupted any minute, because it was almost evening. But she wasn't interrupted. Finally she finished sewing and got out the iron and pressed the new shirt she had been working on. Then she started supper. But still her husband didn't come home. After a very long time she ate supper by herself, but she was worried now and just picked at her food. Much later she finally cried herself to sleep on the living-room couch, because he never came home at all that night.

He did come home the following evening, and when he walked in, she asked him, "Where have you been?"

He looked at her, astonished. "What do you mean?"

"*Where were you last night?*"

He looked even more surprised. "Why do you want to know? Surely you don't expect me to come home *every* night. That's the most ridiculous thing I've heard in a long time. There are thousands of married people who spend time apart. So what's the big deal if I don't come home now and again? We don't have to be that rigid about our marriage. Last night I just didn't *feel* like coming home. I had some more important things to do. I have a busy schedule, you know. And I come home to you most nights. Isn't that enough?''

"No, it's not!" she replied, and started to cry.

"Hey, look," he said more gently. "The trend of our marriage is for me to come home. You shouldn't get upset about the occasional night here and there that I want to spend with one of my other friends. I don't have to come home every night in order for us to stay married. I think it's much more healthy for our marriage not to get into some kind of legalistic routine. Wouldn't you hate to see me come home every night just out of habit? If we don't get into such a rut, we'll have a much more exciting marriage.''

ARE YOU IMPRESSED?

If you are curious about the ending to this little parable, let me assure you, they did *not* live happily ever after! Why? Because marriage involves commitment. And while there may be times when the feelings are high and times when the feelings are low, a good marriage is never based on feeling. It is based on a lifetime commitment to someone you love, and who loves you in return.

We've talked about the prescription for a successful relationship and fellowship with God. We have seen that the basis of the devotional life of the Christian is to take time, alone, at the beginning of each day, to seek Jesus through His Word and through prayer. Just as in marriage, there is commitment involved in the relationship with Christ. Because of that commitment, we will continue to seek Jesus day by day, regardless of our feelings.

Now suppose that you have made the commitment to this relationship with Christ. Suppose that you have determined to set aside prime time in your day for the purpose of getting to know God. What will be the result?

If you make this decision before you have been born again, when you are not yet converted, there are two possible results. In the first place, it may be an uphill trek, for it is only with the new birth that a relish for spiritual things is experienced. But it is possible to begin a relationship with Christ and find that by beholding Jesus and His love, you are brought to conversion.

A second possibility for the unconverted person who makes the commitment to the devotional life is to end up in complete frustration. The factor that makes the difference between the two outcomes is your sense of need. Jesus said, "They that be whole need not a physician, but they that are sick" (Matt. 9:12). It is the sense of need that makes the difference.

AFTER THE NEW BIRTH

For the one who *has* been born again and who makes the commitment to the relationship with Christ there are also two possibilities. The relationship can grow and become ever more meaningful, or it can go sour. Once again, what makes the difference is the sense of need. Before one's conversion the sense of need is often created by the bumps and bruises of life. But what about after conversion? How do we get, and keep, the sense of need? At this point I'd like to add one thing that I didn't include in the basic prescription for a devotional life. I left out Christian witness. And there was a reason for leaving it out until now.

In the first place, in order to be a witness you must have something to tell. Suppose you were called to be a witness in a court of law, and when you had been sworn in and taken your place on the witness stand, the judge said, "Where were you at the time of the crime?"

And you respond, "I was at home in bed, asleep."

"Well, did you hear anything, see anything?"

"No, Your Honor, I slept right through it. I didn't even know anything had happened until the next morning."

"And you're a *witness?*"

They'd throw you out of court!

Sometimes Christian churches have the idea that if they could just get everyone involved in witness and outreach, that would bring revival and reformation and spiritual life. But the very first prerequisite for being a witness is to have something personal to witness to. We cannot be witnesses to hearsay, or grapevine, information. Witness demands personal knowledge and experience. Therefore, true witnessing can begin only after a person has a one-to-one relationship with Christ.

WITNESSING: CAUSE AND RESULT

Yet witnessing is both a cause and a result of Christian life. Or perhaps it would be more accurate to say that witnessing is the result and cause of Christian life, for we cannot witness until we first have something to tell. But as we become involved in witness and outreach toward others, it increases our sense of need, it drives us to our knees, and thus becomes an effective means of causing the devotional relationship with God to continue to be fresh and meaningful. This was God's purpose in giving us a part to act in sharing the good news of the gospel with others.

In our becoming acquainted with God it is vital to spend time in direct communication, in talking to Him and in listening to His voice through His Word. But witnessing is the third way by which we become acquainted—through going places and doing things with Him, through working with Him.

The same principle applies to any relationship. Few friendships are based completely on conversational communication—yet few friendships survive without it. We take time to talk to and listen to the ones we love. But we also become even better acquainted as we work together, travel together, play together. It has been said that there are two tests of a marriage: First, wallpaper the bathroom together. Then, if you're still married, try cleaning out the garage together. If you've ever tried either of these, you should be able to give personal testimony to the fact that it is possible to find out things about your mate when you are doing things together that you might never have known if you had only sat and talked and looked at each other.

WITNESSING IS . . .

Before we go any further on this point, perhaps it is important to discuss briefly what witnessing *is* and what it is *not*. Have you ever had the idea that witnessing is primarily going out to ring doorbells of people you have never seen before and trying to tell them about religion? Have you thought that you would be expected to drop "gospel bombs" by rural mailboxes or pass out pamphlets to the people in the tollbooths when you're traveling? Or have you perhaps been afraid you'd be asked to stop people on the streets or at the airport and try to get them to accept the gospel?

If you have ever felt uneasy at the thought of such activities and been convinced that you're just not the type, welcome to the club. And I have good news for you! Jesus suggested to the man He healed in the country of the Gadarenes that he go home to *his friends* and tell *them* what great things God had done for him (Mark 5:19). He wasn't expected to begin by approaching total strangers or traveling to some distant land. Jesus said instead, "Go home to thy friends." And he was not asked to begin suddenly giving Bible lessons about prophecy and doctrine. He was to tell what Jesus had done for him personally.

On the other hand, people sometimes give the impression that it is not necessary ever to say *anything,* but simply take refuge in being what is called a silent witness. Let's back up a minute to the courtroom again and see how that would work out.

The judge says, "Where were you on the night of the twenty-seventh?"

Silence.

"I said, Where were you on the night of the twenty-seventh?"

More silence.

Finally, just before the judge charges you with contempt of court, you manage to say, "I would like to be simply a silent witness. I think that my mere presence here in the courtroom should indicate where my loyalties lie. I'm not good at speaking, so I'll just be a silent witness."

No, a witness not only has something to say—he *says* it! It is, no doubt, vital to our Christian witness that we are kind and loving and interested in helping those in need. But there are atheists who may do many kind and loving things. In order to be a witness for the Lord Jesus Christ, we must have something to say about Him and His love and what He means to us personally. When telling what great things He has done for us is united with the life of care and concern for the welfare of others, we uplift Jesus.

THE THREE TANGIBLES

Paul says in Philippians 2:12, "Work out your own salvation with fear and trembling." How do you work out your own salvation? What is your part? What can you do? Three things. The study of the Bible and spending time in prayer are the first two. The third is Christian witness. But you really can't become involved in telling what a wonderful Friend you have found in Jesus until you have a meaningful relationship with Him. So Bible study and prayer become an absolute necessity in order to end up with a genuine Christian witness. But it is inevitable that if we do not become involved in Christian witness and outreach and service, the Bible study and prayer will go sour, and we'll end up worse off than we were before we started.

Jesus told a parable in Matthew 25 to illustrate the fact that if we do not become involved in working and sharing with others, we will lose what spirituality we already have. You can read it in verses 14-30. In the conclusion, verse 29, Jesus said, " ' "For to every person who has something, even more will be given, and he will have more than enough; but the person who has nothing, even the little that he has will be taken away from him" ' " (T.E.V.). It is in sharing God's love with others that we keep our own soul alive.

If we do not grow, we will die. That is true in nature, as well as in spiritual life. A plant must either grow or die. One day my wife brought home two rosebushes. We planted them in the best soil. We tried to give them plenty of water. But neither one of them grew. Finally when they looked as though they were dead, we transplanted one into a different spot. It began to grow! We transplanted the other one, too, but that plant was dead. In spite of everything we tried, nothing renewed it. The plant that did not grow died.

Jesus talked about the principles of growth in Mark 8:35: "For whosoever will save his life shall lose it; but whosoever shall lose his life for my sake and the gospel's, the same shall save it." It is in giving to others in service that we grow, and as we grow, spiritual life continues.

REASONS NOT TO WITNESS

There are several common fears that people have that result in their not wanting to get involved in service and outreach. The first is spiritual uncertainty in ourselves. We find it hard to convince others that God will accept them just as they are if we are not yet convinced that He accepts us. We find it difficult to introduce Jesus to others when we don't know Him for ourselves.

A second fear is the fear of failure. We worry that we might not succeed in witnessing effectively. We prefer to leave the witnessing to the "professionals," who we think will know how to do it right. But success or failure has never been our department. We are not to worry ourselves about success. It is only the power of the Holy Spirit that can win hearts.

A third fear that is often expressed is the fear of somehow giving wrong information—of not being enough of a theologian to be able to answer all the questions and arguments that might be raised. Here again, if we are talking of witness in terms of what Jesus has done for us, we should know the answers! It is not required that each Christian become a theologian and student of prophecy and learn the Greek and Hebrew and all the rest of it before he or she can tell someone else about the love and power of Christ.

Another major objection to witnessing is that it takes time. Here again, this objection is often based on the misconception that witnessing is a major addition to our daily schedule, of going out to spend perhaps hours talking to strangers or passing out tracts. But for the one who is in relationship with Jesus and has something to tell, witnessing becomes a way of life. It does not necessarily involve an extra amount of time to speak of Jesus to family and friends in our daily contact with them.

But God has given us a gift of time specifically for the purpose of entering into the joy of working with Him. It is called the Sabbath. One day in seven God gives us time—time to communicate with Him in a special way and time to join Him in service to others. Do you have a friend who has been ill and would welcome a visit, but you just haven't had time to go to see him? God has given you the Sabbath. Is there a neighbor who you know is lonely and you'd like to invite over, but you've been too busy? God has given you the Sabbath. Have you been intending to take your children out into nature or maybe for a picnic by the lake, but you haven't found the time? God has given you the Sabbath. Whether we are sharing God's love with family and friends or reaching out into the world beyond, there is time, every week—God's special answer to the problem of finding time, in our busy schedules, to reach out to others.

In addition, it is God's purpose that witnessing and service become a way of life. There will be, it is true, times of more structured outreach and sharing. But our witness can never be limited to these times alone. In fact, whether we know it or not, we *are* witnesses all day long, in everything we do. By our lives, by our actions, by the very atmosphere that surrounds us, we are giving witness for or against God. When we have a vital relationship with God, it will color all our witnessing, both silent and verbal, and will be used by God to share His love with others within our sphere of influence.

OTHER PROBLEMS IN THE DEVOTIONAL LIFE

In nine cases out of ten, if there has been a time of meaningful communication with God day by day but it has gone sour, it is because of a lack of involvement in outreach and service and sharing with others. But there are some other things that can short-circuit the relationship with God. Let us look briefly at several of these.

One problem that many people encounter is the problem of an irregular devotional life. They spend time with God on occasion and are thrilled with the insights into His love and acceptance that they discover. Then they get busy, and they miss a day or a few days or maybe a week or two. Then usually because of some problem or trouble in their life, they begin again to seek Jesus. But after a few days they are past the crisis and once again find it easy to forget and to neglect. Sometimes people wonder, as they see the lack of spiritual growth that comes from the on-again, off-again relationship, whether God is angry at them for neglecting Him and whether that's why they are punished with the results that come.

But they are forgetting that when we neglect personal communion with God and personal fellowship with Christ, we have an enemy who makes the most of it. In the Bible, where it speaks of God, it also speaks of His enemy, the devil. We are told that our "adversary the devil, as a roaring lion, walketh about, seeking whom he may devour" (1 Peter 5:8). When we neglect fellowship with God, we can be sure that the enemy will do everything he can to keep us from again finding meaning in the relationship with Jesus, for he knows this is our only source of power. He will try to keep us too busy to take time for God. He will bring in all the problems of life. He will wipe us out with temptation and sin, and then tell us that we don't dare come back to Jesus until we have put in a couple of weeks of faithful service. Then ten days later he causes us to fall and fail again. This can go on and on and on until the strongest person becomes discouraged.

Another problem that causes some people to scrap the relationship with God is a misunderstanding of what faith is all about. *Faith* is a very misunderstood word. There are people who think that faith is something you work up, something you generate yourself. But I'd like to propose that faith is never worked up by the person—faith is the gift of God. Paul tells us that clearly.

There are whole churches built on the false premise that faith is something you work on. People have gotten the idea that you must exercise your faith, and that the way to exercise it is to make yourself believe that something is going to happen. They feel that if you can believe strongly enough, what you believe is going to happen will happen.

THE LITTLE GIRL WITH THE UMBRELLA

The story is told of a little girl who came to a church service where people were gathering to pray for rain. The crops were drying up, and they needed rain badly. The little girl came bringing her umbrella. The people smiled at her faith.

But it did rain. And so they said that it rained because the little girl brought her umbrella. And if you have enough nerve and courage to bring your umbrella, it'll cause the rain to come. But the truth is not that it rained because she brought her umbrella, but that she brought her umbrella because she knew it was going to rain. Is there a difference?

Ephesians 2:8 says, "By grace are ye saved through faith; and *that* not of yourselves: it is the gift of God." Faith is a gift from God. You don't work it up. Faith is more than belief. It is more than "taking God at His word," which many Christians have accepted as a definition. Faith is trust—and trust comes from communication and acquaintance with One who is absolutely trustworthy.

A misunderstanding of what faith, or trust, is all about can lead to problems in the relationship with Christ. A false idea of faith leads us to expect Him to act or react in a certain way to our petitions. And when we pray and don't get the answers we are looking for, or when unexpected trial comes into our lives, we give in to the temptation to scrap the whole business.

One time I went to see a man who was a hard customer. I was holding some public meetings in his town, and someone said, "Why don't you invite him to the meetings?" I went to his home, out at the edge of town, and knocked on his door. He opened the door, and when he heard who I was, he said, "Oh, you blankety-blank preachers!" (Only he didn't say *blankety-blank!*)

Then he invited me in—and that didn't make sense! But I

went in and sat down, and he began to unload on me, trying to insult me. One of the things he said was "I have talked to the blankety-blank pillow just as many times as to any blankety-blank preacher, and I never got any blankety-blank answers from either."

He had scrapped his prayer life on the basis of whether or not he got answers. If the only reason you pray is to get answers, you are going to scrap your prayer life sooner or later.

There was a time when I thought that Bible study and prayer were an end in themselves. But then I discovered that these are the great avenues that God has given so we can communicate with Him. If we will make the commitment to communicate with Him through these avenues, we will get to know Him. And when we get to know Him, we will find that trust is awakened spontaneously.

FAITH IS SPONTANEOUS

One of the greatest single symptoms of genuine faith, or trust, is its spontaneity. It is akin to love in this respect. Have you ever tried to make yourself love someone? How did it go? You can't turn love on and off, can you?

One of the most tricky deceptions of the enemy is to get a person to work on anything else except his acquaintance with Jesus. A person says, "I'm interested in religion. I'm interested in becoming a Christian." And the devil says, "Oh, oh!" And he calls together a ways and means committee. It has nothing to do with money. It's ways and means of sidetracking the person from knowing God. The devil says, "If this person is going to insist on trying to become a Christian, then let's get him to work on righteousness." So he begins to whisper in the person's ear, "You've got to be good if you're going to be a Christian. You've got to do what's right. You'd better work on it! Oh—you slipped today. You'd better work harder."

Have you ever tried so hard to go to sleep at night that you woke yourself up? Have you ever fought the devil so hard that you became more like him? If you keep looking at yourself in the mirror, you will soon begin looking more like yourself! By beholding we become changed.

Let me remind you again that we don't work on righteousness. Righteousness comes through Jesus; it is not worked up. Romans 4:4, 5: "To him that worketh is the reward not reckoned of grace, but of debt. But to him that worketh not, but believeth on him that justifieth the ungodly, his faith is counted for righteousness."

This doesn't mean that righteousness doesn't come. But it comes as a gift from God, not as the fruit of our own efforts. When we are finally brought to the realization that righteousness is by faith, then the devil says, "That's right—now you've got it! Work on faith. Make yourself believe. If you believe strongly enough, you'll get the victory, or the answer to prayer you're looking for."

But the devil is a liar—in fact, the Bible says so in John 8:44. The truth is that *both* righteousness and faith come as the result of a relationship with the Lord Jesus Christ. Faith is not an end in itself. It is a means to an end. And it always comes and grows, in its genuine form, from a relationship with Jesus that is firm and alive.

Righteousness does not come to those who seek it. Righteousness comes to those who seek only Jesus. Faith does not come to those who seek it, but to those who seek only Jesus.

I invite you today to accept what it is that produces genuine, saving faith. It is the basis of the entire Christian life. It is the way of salvation. It is in knowing Jesus as your personal friend. And the relationship and fellowship with Jesus will lead you into all the rest of what Jesus has in mind for you, both in this world and in the world to come.

WHY THINGS GO WORSE WHEN SEEKING GOD MORE

One more problem that can cause people to scrap their devotional life, a problem that is so common that it should be dealt with, is that often when we begin to seek a relationship with God, everything goes wrong at once. Now, it doesn't always happen, but it does seem to happen more often than not.

It would make sense, of course, if you were the devil, and you knew that the relationship with Jesus was the entire basis of the Christian life and growth, to do everything you could to discourage the person who was seeking Him. But what perplexed me when it first happened to me was the thought Isn't God big enough to keep this sort of thing from happening?

The answer to this dilemma is a fascinating one and is found in the first two chapters of the book of Job. Let's go to the story, beginning with chapter 1, verses 6 through 8: "Now there was a day when the sons of God came to present themselves before the Lord, and Satan came also among them. And the Lord said unto Satan, Whence comest thou? [Or, Where are you from?]

"Then Satan answered the Lord, and said, From going to and fro in the earth, and from walking up and down in it.

"And the Lord said unto Satan, Hast thou considered my servant Job, that there is none like him in the earth, a perfect and an upright man, one that feareth God, and escheweth [turns away from] evil?"

Satan's contention was "I'm from the earth. I'm in charge down there." God's contention was "You're not in charge of everyone. Have you considered my servant Job?"

"Then Satan answered the Lord, and said, Doth Job fear God for nought [for nothing]? Hast not thou made an hedge about him, and about his house, and about all that he hath on every side? thou hast blessed the work of his hands, and his substance is increased in the land. But put forth thine hand now, and touch all that he hath, and he will curse thee to thy face.

"And the Lord said unto Satan, Behold, all that he hath is in thy power; only upon himself put not forth thine hand.

"So Satan went forth from the presence of the Lord" (verses 9-12).

What was the issue? Satan's charge was that the only reason Job served God was that he got wealth and blessings from God, right? That was his charge. And at least in the case of Job, God saw best in His wisdom to let Satan try to prove his point. So God gave him permission. And Satan came in with all his guns blazing, so to speak, and took away everything Job had.

Now, Job misunderstood. He thought it was God who took away everything he had (verse 21). There has always been a great deal of misunderstanding of God, hasn't there? But in spite of Job's misunderstanding of God, he did not become as one of the foolish ones. He maintained his trust in God. He must have known God well enough to have a basis for trust that could endure even in the face of some misunderstandings.

Let's go on to chapter 2: "Again there was a day when the sons of God came to present themselves before the Lord, and Satan came also among them to present himself before the Lord. And the Lord said unto Satan, From whence comest thou? And Satan answered the Lord, and said, From going to and fro in the earth, and from walking up and down in it.

"And the Lord said unto Satan, Hast thou considered my servant Job, that there is none like him in the earth, a perfect and an upright man, one that feareth God, and escheweth evil? and still he holdeth fast his integrity, although thou movedst me against him, to destroy him without cause.

"And Satan answered the Lord, and said, Skin for skin, yea, all that a man hath will he give for his life. But put forth thine hand now, and touch his bone and his flesh, and he will curse thee to thy face.

"And the Lord said unto Satan, Behold, he is in thine hand; but save his life.

"So Satan went forth from the presence of the Lord, and smote Job with sore boils from the sole of his foot unto his crown" (verses 1-7). And still Job maintained his integrity.

Mrs. Job, however, did not. Job had lost everything he had except his wife. But the devil knew she would be a useful tool in his hands. As soon as he got Mrs. Job he must have sat back and smiled and congratulated his imps, and reminded them that if they kept at it they would get Job as well.

JOB, PART 2

Let's not look at the story of Job as simply a history lesson. It can teach us important truths about why things get worse when we are seeking God more. I would like to suggest that the experience of Job is worked out in every person's life sooner or later. You can experience Job, part 1, part 2, or part 10. It works something like this: Satan knows that all he needs in order to keep us in his ranks is to keep us away from personal fellowship with God. He doesn't care so much what he causes us to do or not do. Often he gloats not so much over what we do wrong as in what we don't do wrong if we keep from wrong through our own strength. Satan evidently arbitrarily chooses to leave some people on the throne, while he pushes others into the gutter. A person can be lost while glorying in his successes if his successes are won in his own strength, apart from Jesus, just as easily as he can be lost while wallowing in his failures.

So Satan probably couldn't care less what he causes us to do or not do as far as evil deeds are concerned. The one thing he chews his fingernails over is whether or not a person is actually coming into fellowship and communion with God. He is worried sick when he sees a person becoming interested in the experience of salvation by faith, for he knows that this is what will defeat him in the long run.

So when we begin to become interested in knowing God, the devil calls his ways and means committee to keep this from happening in your life and in my life. At the same time he shakes his fist at God and makes the same sort of charge he did concerning Job. Satan says to God, "You see this person? The reasons he's searching for You are selfish ones. He wants to get into heaven. He wants to get over his ulcers. He wants to get the peace that he hears other Christians talk about. He wants his problems solved and his prayers answered. He's not seeking You because he loves You. He's seeking You because of what he can get out of You."

Then he tells his imps to come at us with all barrels blazing. I am talking from personal experience, because it takes a thief to know a thief! When I first began to seek a real experience with God, everything caved in. Talk about trouble—physical trouble, financial trouble, family trouble. Not only that, but the devil comes personally with every temptation he can muster and causes us to fall and fail, and sometimes even to live a worse life than before. And in spite of the fact that we are seeking God, spending time in His Word and on our knees, everything caves in.

Now, you know what I did the first time that happened? At the close of the day I said, "Well, *that* didn't work!" The next morning I decided to sleep in.

Guess what happened. I had a good day! Everything went smoothly. I didn't even "sin." At the close of the day I congratulated myself on the fine life I had lived that day. And the devil went back to his ways and means committee, and they all had a laughing session! Their strategy had worked.

I had a student tell me one time, "I quit being a Christian two weeks ago, and I haven't sinned since!" Often we find that at the point we scrap the relationship with Christ, things apparently go better. Our problems seem to cease.

Well, now, right there you would think that the devil would be smart enough to leave well enough alone. But as number one sinner in the universe, Satan has a remarkable lack of self-control. So he goes along for a couple of weeks leaving me alone, and he has me, because I'm not seeking God, not praying, not into the Word of God. But then he comes at me again—just for fun this time. He's not happy just to see a person lost; he'd like to have him in the gutter as well. So when he comes in after a week or two and brings more trouble, it drives me to my knees. Have you ever had it happen? We say, "I guess I do need this experience with God, after all." And we once again begin to seek God. Then the devil gets really nervous. He chews his nails some more, and he complains to his imps and says, "What's the matter with you, anyway?" And once again they come at us with everything they have.

If the devil had been smart enough, he would have left some of us alone, and he would have had us a long time ago. But he continued to needle us until we were driven to God permanently. God can bring some of the devil's maneuvers out to His own glory, can He not?

THE SECRET OF JOB

I hate to admit how many times I went through this sick routine until one day it dawned on me what had been happening. It was Job, part 2. And what was Job's secret? When Job proved before the universe and before the opposing forces in the great controversy between Christ and Satan that he was serving God not for selfish reasons, but because he loved Him, then God could come in with His blessings and cause the devil to flee. And in the end the blessings of Job were doubled.

How does Job, part 2, work out? When the devil makes his charge that our motives for seeking God are selfish, God has to

let the devil try to prove his point until our own motives have
been revealed to ourselves, to the devil, and to the entire
universe. God has always been fair, even in His dealings with
the devil. And the time will come one of these days when every
knee is going to bow and every tongue is going to confess that
God has been fair and just (see Phil. 2:10, 11). And Satan
himself will go to his knees and admit that God has never
overstepped Himself.

All right, so I begin to seek God, and Satan says, "He's
seeking You only for selfish reasons. And I was kicked out of
heaven for selfishness. You can't help him anymore." God is in
a corner. The only one who can prove whether God is right or the
devil is right is you or I.

What happened at the end of that first day when everything
went wrong and I said, "Well, that didn't work," and slept in
the next morning? On whose side did I cast my vote? I proved
the devil right. When things didn't go as I'd planned, I forgot
about seeking God, and Satan was absolutely correct in my case.
When it finally dawned on my mind what was happening, I
realized why it was that God had to let him be hard on me. I
realized that my motives for seeking God had been wrong.

But I can't change my motives. The selfish heart cannot
change itself. There is only one place where motives can be
changed, and that is at the feet of Jesus.

SEEKING GOD FOR THE RIGHT REASONS

So when we see the issue, we go to our knees and say,
"Please, God, I see my problem. Will You give me Your grace
to change my motives and to begin to seek You for Your sake,
instead of for my own?" Wouldn't you like to seek God for His
sake, instead of for your own sake? Wouldn't you like to be able
to seek God as a response of love, because of what Jesus has
already done for us at the cross? Wouldn't you like to keep

seeking fellowship and communion with Heaven regardless of what is happening in your life, good or bad? When you do that, you begin to experience the rest of the story of Job being fulfilled in your life.

One day you see God coming to the devil, and He says, "How are things going?" (If you will, forgive me for putting words into God's mouth.)

The devil says, "I'm giving him everything I've got."

And God says, "I know. I've been watching. But he is still seeking communion with Heaven, isn't he?"

The devil begins to fidget.

And God says, "Could it be possible that this person is seeking Me because of what My Son has done? Could it be that he is seeking Me because of love, rather than for selfish reasons?"

And about this time the devil fades away into the distance. He has nothing more to say.

PROVING GOD RIGHT

God's contention was that Job loved Him and that that was why he was faithful. And Job proved that God was right. It is my privilege today to prove that God is right again. God help us to seek Him because we love Him, and to surrender our selfish motives to Him. It is only then that God can come in with all the blessings and power from heaven that He longs to bring.

Obedience. How? Why?
And what happens when I
fail?

Which comes first, victory
or peace? How can I keep
from sinning?

DAY 4

"When I was a little boy, I sat me down to cry
   Because my little brother had the biggest piece of pie."
   My father used to repeat that bit of verse to my brother and
me on occasion. I remember that one year just before Christmas
some nice church members gave us boys each a bag of
Christmas candy. It was hard candy, the kind that seems to stay
in your mouth for hours.

   My parents were immediately concerned. They didn't want
us to ruin our teeth or our stomachs, and so they made a rule.
Only one piece of candy at a time, and that at mealtime. No

candy between meals. I was 6 years old, and my brother was 8. And those rules were too much for a little guy, so I got into my bag of candy between meals. When my father heard about it, he promptly destroyed my candy.

At that point I became very concerned about my brother's health, and decided to help him out by dumping his bag of candy down the toilet!

As a result of my intervention in his behalf, diplomatic relations around our house were not too good for a while. My brother still loves to tell the story every chance he gets! But why do we do this kind of thing? What is it that drives us to war, in the extreme manifestation, or to apparently innocent parlor games at the other end of the spectrum—or to football and baseball somewhere in between? Why do we rally so completely around the question of who's going to win, who's going to be on top, who's going to be first?

It all began with sin, didn't it? Lucifer, covering cherub, the "son of the morning," said in his heart, "I will ascend into heaven, I will exalt my throne above the stars of God: I will sit also upon the mount of the congregation, in the sides of the north: I will ascend above the heights of the clouds; I will be like the most High." You can read about it in Isaiah 14:12-14. And he carried this same temptation to our first parents, in the Garden of Eden. Genesis 3:5: "Ye shall be as gods." Sin began with taking glory to self that belonged to God the Creator alone, and much of our lives we spend in contention over who's the greatest. We have our recreation, our fun, over it. We see it in the business world, in the neighborhood, and at times even in the church. And in its final struggle it brings death.

As we have noticed earlier, the basic issue in all sin is separation from God, which results and is manifest in this insatiable desire to be first, to be the greatest. This self-centeredness is the basis of all of the sinful deeds and thoughts and actions that we see in our lives.

Sometimes people have thought that when they experienced the new birth, they would be totally and completely and forever finished with self-centeredness and sin and its resulting disobedience. And they were astonished and appalled, the week after the week before, to discover some of the same sins and problems and failures in their lives as before they ever entered into a relationship with Christ. And all too often this has resulted in the newly converted Christian becoming discouraged, scrapping the relationship with Christ and waiting for the next revival or altar call or spiritual awakening. But conversion has never been a guarantee of instant and absolute perfection, and thus the question of how the growing Christian relates to falling and failing and sinning is a very practical, if painful, subject.

HOW JESUS TREATED KNOWN SINNERS

Is it possible for saints to sin? Is it possible to sin and know that you are sinning, and keep doing what you are doing wrong, and still be a Christian? How does Jesus treat saints who sin? This is a practical question, and has an answer that is exciting and encouraging.

But let's try to build our case as we notice from Scripture how Jesus treated sinning Christians. The text is Mark 9, beginning with verse 33: "And he [Jesus] came to Capernaum: and being in the house he asked them [the disciples], What was it that ye disputed among yourselves by the way? But they held their peace: for by the way they had disputed among themselves, who should be the greatest."

You see Jesus and His disciples traveling down the dusty roads toward Capernaum. Jesus had set His face toward Jerusalem, and the disciples were certain that He was going there to set up His kingdom, which they expected to be an earthly kingdom. But they had some unfinished business. They hadn't yet settled who was to be president of the class, who was to be prime minister, who was going to be chancellor of the exchequer, who was to be the greatest.

So as they walked along toward Capernaum they were trying to take care of their unfinished business. They knew their strife was wrong, and so they lagged behind Jesus. When they reached Capernaum, they were so far behind Him that He could not hear their conversation, and when they were alone in the house, Jesus asked them what they had been talking about along the way.

This teaches us something very interesting about sinning. It is difficult to sin in the presence of Jesus. Have you discovered that? In fact, most people, even the weakest people, would admit that it's difficult to sin in the presence of someone you love and respect highly. Most sinning has to be carried out in the absence of those we love and respect. Somehow we have to feel that we're away from God, away from Christ Jesus, in order to continue in deliberate, known sinning.

And so you see the disciples lagging behind Jesus, hoping to hide from Him the topic of conversation that they found so absorbing. But when they arrived in Capernaum at the house where they were to be staying, Jesus sent Peter off on a strange mission down to the seashore, to the bank . . . to the *bank!* An interesting bank, as you may recall. A fish's mouth. And while Peter was gone, Jesus asked the rest of the disciples a question. Apparently He had more than one reason for sending Peter off to the bank! He didn't want Peter around when He came in with His home thrust. He wanted the other disciples to have a chance to think without Peter answering all the questions first.

So Jesus sent Peter away, and then said to the disciples, "What were you talking about on the way to Capernaum?"

They began to kick their feet in the dust, and fidget. They didn't answer. Verse 34 says, "They held their peace." It was a good time for them to hold their peace! When I was asked what happened to my brother's bag of Christmas candy, I held my peace too! But Jesus continued to press His question, and at long last one of the disciples said, ''Well, uh, ahem! We were wondering, er, who is going to be the greatest in the kingdom.''

"GIVE ME ANOTHER TWELVE!"

Now Jesus' life had been a life of humility. Jesus had emptied Himself, and ''made himself of no reputation,'' according to Philippians 2:7. He who had had the homage and worship of all the heavenly hosts had come to this earth and been born in a humble stable. He who had been rich beyond all imagination had become poor, that we through His poverty might become rich (2 Cor. 8:9). Again and again He had tried to help the disciples understand that real greatness is based upon humility. But they hadn't gotten the message.

At this point I suppose it might have been easy for Jesus to say, ''Get out of My sight, you miserable twelve. Give Me another twelve; I'm starting over!'' But instead He called them unto Him and said, ''If any man desire to be first, the same shall be last of all, and servant of all. And he took a child, and set him in the midst of them: and when he had taken him in his arms, he said unto them, Whosoever shall receive one of such children in my name, receiveth me: and whosoever shall receive me, receiveth not me, but him that sent me'' (Mark 9:35-37). He used a little child to illustrate what the kingdom of heaven is really like.

He was kind to His disciples. He was patient with them. He didn't condemn them. He gave them His lessons, and when they didn't learn, He continued teaching. And above all He continued walking with them. He continued fellowshiping with them. He continued eating with them, traveling with them, working with them, trusting them with His work and His mission.

GUILTY OF THE *WORST* SIN

From this lesson in Scripture we have evidence of how Jesus treated His disciples when they sinned. What was the sin? It was the sin of pride. Oh, we say, everybody has a bit of pride. That's what our world is based on. That's what makes it fun to play games like Monopoly or Pit or Uno. And sanctification is the work of a lifetime; just before we die, maybe we'll get on top of that little problem of pride. But no, pride is the worst sin. It was the sin of pride that started the whole mess in this world in the first place. And while it is true that in God's estimation, just as in ours, there are degrees of sin, He has a different scale. Pride is the most offensive to God, because it is most contrary to His nature.

This sin, of which the disciples were guilty, was one of the worst sins, if not *the* worst. It was sin; it was *bad* sin. And they knew it was wrong, because they saved their indulgence in this sin until Jesus was out of earshot. And yet they continued doing it. In fact, they continued in this sin the whole three years they were with Christ. They were still at it in the upper room on the night before the crucifixion. And so it qualifies as known sin, continuing sin, habitual sin, cherished sin, persistent sin, presumptuous sin—you name it. The disciples were guilty of the worst sin.

I can remember during my teen years hearing someone make a point that the only kind of sins that God forgives is sins of ignorance. And he came up with a verse or two from the Old Testament, trying to prove from the sacrificial system that there were provisions only for sins of ignorance. And this just about finished me off, because all my sins were not sins of ignorance. How about yours?

There are some scholars who say that "sinneth not" in 1 John 3:6 means we will not commit any known sin. We might slip, we might miss the mark, but we won't sin intentionally. So you get the impression that the kind of sins God can forgive are the ones you accidentally slip into. But there are too many people whose sinning is far more severe than that and who can find no comfort in that approach.

But in the experience of the disciples we can learn how Jesus treated sinning sinners who knew they were sinning and who kept on sinning.

WERE THE DISCIPLES CONVERTED?

At this point someone might say, "The problem with these disciples was that they were not converted." Don't tell me that! I need to remind you that these disciples were the ones who were casting out devils and cleansing the lepers and healing the sick and raising the dead. God doesn't normally give power to unconverted people to do that. When the seventy came back from their mission, rejoicing in the power to cast out devils, Jesus said, "But rather rejoice, because your names are written in heaven" (Luke 10:20). And John 3 says you can't even see the kingdom of heaven unless you are born again. So by inference we must accept the premise that the twelve disciples were converted.

It is true that Jesus said to Peter the night before the crucifixion, "When thou art converted, strengthen thy brethren" (chap. 22:32). But we forget that conversion is a daily matter—and that reconversion for Peter is what's being talked about here. After Peter's denial of Jesus, he needed to be converted anew and repent of his sin. But in the upper room, before the denial, when Peter surrendered to Jesus to allow Him to wash his feet, he was clean. Jesus said so in John 13:10.

So we cannot simply pass off this problem of the known sinning of the disciples as a lack of conversion. How, then, does Jesus treat disciples who are guilty of known sinning? He made

His classic statement in Matthew 12:31: "All manner of sin . . . shall be forgiven unto men." Is that good news?

THE UNPARDONABLE SIN

What about the unpardonable sin? That same passage in Matthew 12 tells us about it. But wait a minute. If *all* manner of sin shall be forgiven, that would have to include the unpardonable sin, too, wouldn't it? Jesus said, "If we confess our sins, he is faithful and just to forgive us our sins, and to cleanse us from all unrighteousness" (1 John 1:9). So Jesus is willing and able to pardon *all* sin, isn't He? He says that all manner of sin shall be forgiven. Then what is the unpardonable sin? The only sin that would not be pardoned would be the one I don't ask pardon for, that I don't repent of. The unpardonable sin is just that simple. Let's circle it in red and green and orange and purple that *"all manner of sin . . . shall be forgiven unto men,"* including known sin, including habitual sin, including persistent sin, including the worst of sins, such as pride.

And if Jesus made it clear that all manner of sin shall be forgiven, and if He forgave the disciples and continued to walk with them even after they persistently had committed the worst sin, then Jesus must have provision and must be able and willing to forgive all lesser sins, such as murder and stealing and adultery, right?

NO CONDEMNATION

The Biblical principle is that "God sent not his Son into the world to condemn the world; but that the world through him might be saved" (John 3:17).

To the adulterous woman whom scribes and Pharisees had dragged to Jesus He gave the great two-pronged answer that is good for anyone caught in the trap of sin. He said, "I don't condemn you," but that's not all He said. What else did He say?

"Go, and sin no more" (John 8:11). There you have the perfect balance.

Often when we find someone whom we love in trouble or in sin, we say, "That's all right; I don't condemn you." And we forget the last part. God loves sinners, but He hates sin. God has provided forgiveness for weak, immature, growing Christians, and He has also provided power to overcome. As we are learning how to appropriate that power in our lives, He continues to walk with us. Jesus sees a man beside the pool. He says, "Sin no more." There is power available. But it is the acceptance of Jesus and the love of Jesus and the relationship with Jesus that bring with them the power to sin no more. It is the presence of Jesus that makes it hard to sin. That's why it is absolutely a necessity for any sinning sinner to be able to count on the presence, the continuing presence, of Jesus.

The greatest need of any young person who is striving to overcome but who is having problems falling and failing and sinning is to know that someone loves him. The only one who grows out of his mistakes is the one who knows he's loved and accepted while he's making them. And does this lead to license? No, it is only this loving relationship, this continuing relationship with Jesus, that leads to victory.

PEACE BRINGS RELEASE

For a long time I thought that if I could somehow overcome my faults and sins and failures, then I'd have peace. It was a real breakthrough to discover that when I had peace, then I could for the first time begin to overcome my faults and sins and failures. It is only when we know by personal experience that Jesus does not condemn us, that He accepts us just as we are, that we gain peace—and that is the beginning of the changes in our lives.

There are four texts that taken together show the truths of forgiveness, love, and obedience so beautifully. The first is found in Matthew 18:21, 22: "Then came Peter to him, and said, Lord, how oft shall my brother sin against me, and I forgive him? till seven times? Jesus saith unto him, I say not unto thee, Until seven times: but, Until seventy times seven."

It was the custom among the Jews in the days of Christ to forgive three times. Peter in an attempt to be generous suggested forgiving twice that, and one more for good measure, bringing the number to seven, the "perfect" number. But Jesus' reply was that seven times isn't nearly enough. Keep forgiving until seventy times seven. And what do we understand that to mean? Are we to keep a ledger and forgive exactly 490 times? No, He was saying that our forgiveness should be unlimited.

Would God ask us to be more forgiving than He is? The answer is obviously No. So this reply of Jesus teaches us that God's forgiveness is unlimited.

The next passage is found in Luke 17:3-5: "If thy brother trespass against thee, rebuke him; and if he repent, forgive him. And if he trespass against thee seven times in a day, and seven times in a day turn again to thee, saying, I repent; thou shalt forgive him. And the apostles said unto the Lord, Increase our faith."

Sometimes a pastor is called upon to settle people's differences. One time I received a phone call from a parishioner who was upset because the neighbor's horse had run through his petunias. My first response was to try to keep from laughing! But then I said, "Call the cops!"

This was perhaps an unfortunate answer. As I reflected on it later, I thought of this passage in Luke. I should have said, "If the horse runs through your petunias six more times today, you should still forgive him."

What would you say if your neighbor's horse had been through your petunias seven times in one day and the neighbor came again for the seventh time to say "I'm sorry"? You know what I'd say? I'd say, "Prove it! Lock up your wretched horse!"

But the major premise is that if Jesus told us to forgive our brother seven times in the same day, God would do no less. God would not ask us to do something that He was unwilling to do. And here again we see that God's forgiveness is unlimited.

How long has it been since you went to God at the end of the day after falling and failing seven times that day, and really believed that you were forgiven? That's hard, isn't it? Because human beings don't think that way. That is not human; that is divine.

When you talk about this kind of forgiveness, there's always someone who gets nervous and says, "You're going to do away with the need for obedience. You're going to bring in license. You're going to get people to play fast and loose with God's grace."

But here we add a third text, Luke 7:40-43. The setting is the feast at Simon's house. Mary comes in—the one whom Simon had led into sin. She anoints the feet of Jesus, and Simon is upset. He has the gall to condemn Mary as a sinner. In his own mind he says, verse 39, "This man, if he were a prophet, would have known who and what manner of woman this is that toucheth him: for she is a sinner."

But Jesus knows his thoughts and says, "Simon, I have somewhat to say unto thee." And Jesus tells a simple story that only Simon understands.

"There was a certain creditor which had two debtors: the one owed five hundred pence, and the other fifty. And when they had nothing to pay, he frankly forgave them both. Tell me therefore, which of them will love him most?

"Simon answered and said, I suppose that he, to whom he forgave most.

"And he said unto him, Thou hast rightly judged."

So you come up with the conclusion that the more you are

forgiven, the more you love. It's a universal and timeless principle.

And then we need to add just one more text, John 14:15: "'If you love me, you *will* obey my commandments'" (T.E.V.). This means that when we come to understand God's forgiveness, we find that it does not lead to license or cheap grace; it leads to obedience.

FORGIVENESS, RELATIONSHIP, OBEDIENCE

With our human limitations we find it hard to really accept such unlimited forgiveness. It is only as we continue to seek Jesus, to learn to know and trust Him more, that we come to experience that which we can recognize in theory—the love and forgiveness of God. When we love Him, we will obey, but even though we are growing in love and trust and fellowship with Him, often we take ourselves out of His hands. It is then that we fall and fail and sin, and need once again to come to Him for repentance—even seven times in a single day.

So it is possible for the growing Christian to discover that he has a known sin going on in his life and at the same time a continuing relationship with Jesus. This is the conclusion we get from the scriptures we have considered in this chapter. The disciples had a relationship with God going on and a known sin going on in their lives at the same time. But as you study you see a further conclusion. Even though it is possible to have a relationship with God going on and a sin going on at the same time, sooner or later one or the other is going to go.

Now, Judas was the smart one of the disciples. He was a fast thinker. And he got the message. He understood this principle, that sooner or later either the sin is going to go or the relationship with Jesus is going to go.

And he said, "I don't want my sin to go." So he deliberately scrapped the relationship in favor of the sin.

Now we have come to the real issue in cherished sin, presumptuous sin, highhanded sin—the kind of sin that gives evidence that we are on dangerous ground, exceedingly dangerous ground. When we choose to scrap the relationship with Jesus or refuse the relationship with Jesus in favor of the sin, then we are in peril.

Perhaps you have met people who did not want to get too religious because they were afraid their lives would change. Perhaps you've met religious people who didn't want to go any further in their relationship with Christ because they didn't want any more changes in their life style. This was Judas. But the other disciples stayed with Jesus. Nothing could take them from His side.

A classic example of the opposite of Judas is John the Beloved. John had just as bad traits as Judas. But John was the man who was always there. John was one of the first disciples to follow Christ. He was there to hear Jesus preaching. He was there to see the miracles. He was there in the Garden, in the court of Caiaphas, at the cross, and at the tomb. John was the man who was always there. But he had problems. He joined his brother in requesting permission to call down fire on the Samaritan village. He, his brother, and his mother went to Christ to solicit a place of favor in His kingdom, one brother at the right hand of Jesus and the other at the left. He was a son of thunder. But he continued to choose to stay with Jesus, and proved in the end that if you continue the relationship with Jesus, sooner or later your sin is going to go. That's the way it works. That's the only way it works.

We see John years later. He's the only one left now; all the other disciples have suffered martyrs' deaths. John is on the Isle of Patmos, and he writes Jesus' own message. He has written letters that have said things such as this: "Beloved, let us love one another: for love is of God. . . . He that loveth not knoweth not God; for God is love'' (1 John 4:7, 8). There's been a change in John—he has been transformed by grace.

Perhaps earlier he had received a visit from some of his friends of past times, and they said to him, ''John, you've changed!''

And John may have looked at them and said, ''Who, me?'' Because the people who are changed are the last ones to know about it and the last ones to advertise it. But God's grace has been doing its work.

THE CONTINUING RELATIONSHIP

May I remind you that if you continue to know Jesus as your personal friend day by day, if you become meaningfully involved with Him in your private life, if nothing can take you from His side, then you will join John the Beloved in a transformation of character that will be unobtrusive, and imperceptible to you. But your friends will probably know it. And whatever sin you're struggling with, whether it's known or unknown, whether it's habitual or cherished or any of the other kinds, it will ultimately fade away.

Sometimes we get impatient and try to put timetables on Christian growth and victory and overcoming. But we'd better not! That's God's business; that's the Holy Spirit's work. The disciples were transformed gradually, first the blade, then the ear, then the full corn in the ear. And so long as the relationship with Christ continues, that relationship of love has its own built-in safeguard against license. The deeper the relationship with Jesus, the further we go from license, or playing cheap and loose with God's grace. I'm thankful today for the way Jesus treated known sinners. It brings hope and comfort to the struggling, growing Christian.

And if it is true that we are transformed through the continued relationship with Christ, then that gives us a major

clue as to the how-to of obedience. We are transformed by
grace, through the continuing relationship with Christ—not
through our own struggles and resolutions and efforts in fighting
sin and the devil.

For a long time in the Christian faith, many have held two
incompatible beliefs: on the one hand, that we can keep God's
commandments, that we can overcome, that we can have
victory over sin; and on the other hand, that we need God's *help*,
but that we're supposed to work hard on our own obedience.

There are some today who have become so frustrated with
the best obedience they have been able to produce in their own
strength that they have decided to scrap the belief in victory and
overcoming altogether. Yet this is not what we find taught in
Scripture. The disciples sinned and failed and fell again and
again, yes. But there is more to the story than that! Through the
continuing relationship with Christ they were changed into His
image and became more than conquerors through Him who
loved them.

While it is true that our acceptance with God is not based
upon our obedience, and while it is true that His forgiveness is
unlimited, these in no way discredit the truth that God has power
available to keep us from sinning.

It is good news to come to the realization that justification is
by faith alone, and have complete confidence in our acceptance
before God, based totally upon what Jesus has already done in
our behalf. It is good news to learn that His forgiveness is
unlimited and that He has infinite patience with us as we grow in
grace. But it is possible to go further and to accept the truth that
obedience and victory and overcoming are available and can
become realities in our lives today. It is good news to learn that
obedience is by faith alone, just as forgiveness is by faith alone.
Paul said it a long time ago, in Colossians 2:6: "As ye have
therefore received Christ Jesus the Lord, so walk ye in him."

REASONS WHY OBEDIENCE COMES BY FAITH ALONE

Now I'd like to list briefly eight Bible reasons why obedience can come by faith alone and not by your own efforts.

1. Because the Bible says so. Is that a good enough argument? In Romans 1:17 Paul says, "The just shall live by faith." Who are the just? They are the ones who have accepted of God's justifying grace, right? And here the Bible tells us that the just, those who have been justified, shall *live* by faith as well.

2. Obedience can come by faith alone because of the nature of mankind. We spent some time discussing this in Day 1. Romans 5:19 says that by one man's sin many were made sinners. And John 3 says that unless we are born again, we cannot see the kingdom of heaven. If it is true that "all our [own] righteousnesses are as filthy rags," as Isaiah 64:6 reminds us, then obedience would have to come from total dependence upon another Power. We couldn't do any of it ourselves, because of our very nature.

3. Obedience can come by faith alone because of the nature of surrender. As we studied in Day 2, surrender means giving up on ourselves (Romans 9 and 10). If we have given up on our own ability, then we must depend upon the power of Another. It is impossible to be trying hard to obey, and give up on ever being able to obey, both at the same time. Giving up negates the possibility of trying hard to accomplish. When we give up, or surrender, we are placing ourselves in total dependence upon God.

4. Obedience comes by faith alone because of the fact that God wants us to be *controlled* by Him. Romans 6 talks about it. We have two options in this world, two possibilities, of who can be in control of our lives. Either God is in control, or the devil is in control. There is no middle ground. The only control we have is in choosing which of the two powers we want to control us.

God's control is the control of love, and as we surrender to His loving control, we *will* become obedient.

5. Obedience can come by faith alone because of the nature of repentance. Repentance is not our own work, but a gift (Acts 5:31). Do you know the classic definition of *repentance?* What *is* repentance? It's sorrow for sin and turning away from it. So if repentance is a gift and if repentance is sorrow for sin and turning away from it, then turning away from sin must be a gift as well, right? It's not something we achieve; it's something we receive.

6. Obedience comes by faith alone because of the fact that obedience is the *fruit* of faith. John 15 is the teaching of Jesus on this point, and He made it clear that obedience is a fruit. Fruit is the result of something else. You don't get fruit by trying hard to produce fruit—you get fruit from the Vine. If we are connected to the Vine, we *will* produce fruit, spontaneously, naturally.

7. Obedience comes by faith alone because of Jesus' mighty example. Jesus did His works and lived His life through power from above Him (John 14:10), rather than from power within. He came to this world not only to die for us, to pay the penalty for sin, but also to show us how to live by dependence upon a Higher Power. Jesus lived His life of obedience by faith alone, and He became the greatest argument in showing that we are invited to live as He did, in obedience by faith.

8. Obedience can come by faith alone because of the fact that we are offered *rest* in living the Christian life, as well as rest from the guilt of sin. Let's look at this last point in a little more detail. Hebrews 4:9 talks about it: "There remaineth therefore a rest to the people of God." (Notice this is for God's people—those who have already accepted Him and become His children.)

Most of us know what it's like to be tired physically. And most of us also know what it's like to be tired spiritually. Let's face it. All of us in every generation have struggled with the burden of holiness. And at times there's not much difference between the burden of holiness and the burden of sin. We often find the Christian life to be like climbing a steep hill with a heavy pack on our back. But Hebrews 4 offers rest to the people of God.

Let's notice several other passages that talk about rest. Revelation 14:11, of all places, in the last message of the three mighty angels: "They have no rest day nor night, who worship the beast and his image, and whosoever receiveth the mark of his name." Well, you say, that's talking about the final destruction of the wicked at the end, in the lake of fire. But wait a minute. There's more to it than simply the prophetic and historic understanding.

Jesus said, "Come unto me, . . . and I will give you rest" (Matt. 11:28). Then if people have no rest day nor night, who worship the beast and his image," the reason is that they are not coming to Jesus, right?

And there's another verse in this passage in Revelation 14 that has a very interesting spiritual meaning. Verse 13: "I heard a voice from heaven saying unto me, Write, Blessed are the dead which die in the Lord from henceforth: Yea, saith the Spirit, that they may rest from their labours; and their works do follow them." Now, I know this has something to do with cemeteries and tombstones and those who die in faith looking forward to the second coming of Jesus. But take another look. There is spiritual meaning here too. "Blessed are the dead which die in the Lord." Have you ever heard of death to self, through Christ? "That they may rest from their labours"—"Come unto me, all ye that labour and are heavy laden, and I will give you rest." "And their works do follow."

And Hebrews 4 talks about rest again: "For he that is entered into his rest, he also hath ceased from his own works, as God did from his'' (verse 10). *When* did God rest from His works? At Creation, right? And that was when He gave the seventh day as a memorial, a sign, to remind us of His creative work. We are invited here in Hebrews 4 to enter into the Sabbath rest. Of what is the Sabbath a sign? Sanctification. Exodus 31:13 talks about it. Ezekiel 20:12, 20 talks about it. The Sabbath is a sign of the God who sanctifies His people. The truth about God's day of rest and the truth about rest from our own efforts to overcome are closely connected.

REST FOR THE WEARY SINNER, REST FOR THE WEARY SAINT

There are three kinds of rest referred to in Hebrews 4: rest from working for acceptance and pardon with God (verses 2, 3), rest from working to overcome the enemy (verses 9, 10), and rest from working to get to heaven, or enter the Promised Land (verse 6). It is possible to accept rest on one level and not on another.

Many people have accepted God's rest in terms of their hope of eternal life, and they trust in Christ's finished work in their behalf. But at the same time it is possible to still be battling and struggling to live the Christian life. You can begin to feel that even though the down payment is free, the monthly payments are going to wipe you out. And you begin to think that this gift of salvation is pretty expensive after all.

But I invite you today to enter into God's rest, to cease from your own works in trying to obey and overcome and be victorious. If we will continue to seek personal fellowship with Him, God will lead us to the rest that is symbolized by the Sabbath rest.

HOW TO OBEY

I will try to put all this in the simplest possible terms. If you enter into a relationship with the Lord Jesus Christ and continue that relationship with Him from now until He comes again, He will do the rest. That's the simplest answer to the question of how to obey. Philippians 1:6 says, "He which hath begun a good work in you will perform it until [carry it forward to] the day of Jesus Christ." Forgiveness is a gift, salvation is a gift, and obedience is a gift, all to be received through continuing fellowship and communion with the One who is the giver.

Genuine obedience can be understood and experienced only by the committed Christian. It is not simply another self-help, behavior modification, or positive-thinking approach that offers outward change for those who are strong-willed enough to pull it off. Obedience by faith alone comes only from the heart and can come only to the one who is in day-by-day communication with Jesus Christ.

You can choose to continue this relationship with God day by day, and the result of knowing Jesus will be the obedience that comes by faith alone. It is good news what God wants to do in us and through us to glorify His name before the world and before the universe.

*Christian growth. From
baby Christian to maturity.
How does it happen?*

*The great divide: those
who know God, and those who
don't know God.*

DAY 5

We were just married, and I was eager to do everything to please my wife. I spent a great deal of time and effort trying to do everything just right to please her. I even became involved in the household duties. But I put the wrong wax on the floor and had to spend a lot of time getting that off. I tried to do the dishes, but broke some of our new wedding presents. I even tried to do some of the ironing, but I burned a hole in her favorite dress. When I made breakfast, I turned the dial too high on the toaster and not only burned the toast black but burned out the elements in the toaster, too. I ended up spending my breakfast time scraping charcoal off the toast into the sink. I tried sewing on some buttons, but sewed the front of her dress to the back of her dress.

She kept wanting to talk. She kept wanting to spend time with me in communication. But I had a lot of things to do. I was scraping toast, repairing the toaster, and removing wax! So I didn't have time just to talk and be with her.

I hope you realize by now that this is a parable! But it is possible to become so involved in trying to do things to please someone that you forget that the thing that pleases him or her most is sitting down and talking. And our efforts to please are going to end in disaster if we try to accomplish that which we are unable to do.

Yet how often in our relationship with Jesus Christ we find ourselves in the same shoes as the Galatians, to whom the apostle Paul wrote, "How can you be so foolish! You began by God's Spirit; do you now want to finish by your own power?" (Gal. 3:3, T.E.V.). How easy it is to slip back into the legalistic approach to Christianity and discover in practice, if not in theory, that the fellowship with Christ has once again taken a back seat while we work and struggle to do what's right, once again trying to save ourselves.

Paul had to remind the early Christians repeatedly that the work that God had begun in their lives *He* would carry forward to the end (Phil. 1:6). He told them, "As ye have therefore received Christ Jesus the Lord, *so walk ye in him*" (Col. 2:6). "Now the just shall *live* by faith: but if any man draw back, my soul shall have no pleasure in him. But we are not of them who draw back unto perdition; but of them that believe to the saving of the soul" (Heb. 10:38, 39). "Looking unto Jesus the author and *finisher* of our faith" (chap. 12:2).

It is never enough simply to begin a relationship with Christ. It is not enough to accept once of His pardoning grace. Without the continuing relationship with Him, the initial receiving of

Christ will never be sufficient for salvation. There is far more to marriage than saying "I do." Getting married is important, but staying married is equally important. Consider a few examples of the continuing-relationship principle as stated in Jesus' own words: "No man, having put his hand to the plough, and looking back, is fit for the kingdom of God" (Luke 9:62). "Because iniquity shall abound, the love of many shall wax cold. But he that shall endure unto the end, the same shall be saved" (Matt. 24:12, 13). "If ye *continue* in my word, then are ye my disciples indeed" (John 8:31).

But let's turn to John 15 for Jesus' most complete discussion of the need for continued relationship with Him, spending time with Him in the vineyard.

ABIDING IN THE VINE

Jesus says, "I am the true vine, and my Father is the husbandman. Every branch in me that beareth not fruit he taketh away: and every branch that beareth fruit, he purgeth it, that it may bring forth more fruit. Now ye are clean through the word which I have spoken unto you. Abide in me, and I in you. As the branch cannot bear fruit of itself, except it abide in the vine; no more can ye, except ye abide in me. I am the vine, ye are the branches: He that abideth in me, and I in him, the same bringeth forth much fruit: for without me ye can do nothing" (verses 1-5).

In this analogy we have first of all the vine, who is Jesus. He says, "I am the *true* vine." In Old Testament analogy Israel was supposed to have been the vine; but they proved to be an unfruitful vine, and so there is a new application, a new interpretation of the vine, through Jesus' words in this chapter. Israel was supposed to have been God's people, but one of their problems was that they felt secure because of their connection with the nation of Israel. The modern analogy would be those who think of the vine as the church and who think that as long as their names are enrolled on the church books, they are assured of eternal life. But Jesus said, *"I* am the true vine." He is speaking here of relationship and connection and communion with Him, not merely of belonging to some church organization.

These words in John 15 were spoken by Jesus just after the upper room experience. Jesus and His disciples were on their way to the Garden of Gethsemane. As they walked along, apparently they passed a vineyard. Jesus pointed to a grapevine that was visible in the moonlight, and used it to teach His disciples by means of this parable.

Have you ever looked closely at a grapevine? Do you think it's beautiful? I don't mean during the summer, when the branches are all in foliage. I mean during the winter, when you can see the vine itself. It's ugly! It looks like a root out of dry ground, doesn't it? It is brown, and knotted, and crooked, and looks as if it were never to live again. It can remind us of the One of whom it was said, "He shall grow up . . . as a root out of a dry ground" (Isa. 53:2). Jesus' beauty was internal rather than external. Verse 2 also says that "when we shall see him, there is no beauty that we should desire him." His beauty came from within, and from His connection with His Father, the husbandman in the parable.

Obviously we are the branches in the story, and it's amazing to discover that the branches often appear more beautiful than the vine, with their green leaves in spring and summer and their bright colors in the fall. That which comes from the vine to the branches results in beauty that apparently Jesus Himself is willing to contribute to His followers, while He stands in the background.

TWO KINDS OF BRANCHES

Notice that there are two kinds of branches in this John 15

parable—two kinds of branches that are "in the vine." Verse 2: "Every branch *in me* that beareth not fruit he taketh away." Does this mean it is possible to have a branch *in Him* that doesn't bear fruit? That's what it says. It doesn't say every branch that pretends to be a true branch or every branch that is connected to the church; it says, "Every branch in me . . ."

So it is possible to be in relationship with Him and not bear fruit, at least for a short while. Perhaps Judas was an example of this. It is obvious that he did not bear fruit and was taken away. Apparently Judas was never fully surrendered to Christ, but he did have the privilege, along with the other eleven, of casting out devils, healing the sick, and raising the dead through the power of Christ. It is possible for a person to become a Christian, to be genuinely converted, to be in the Vine, in Christ, but not to stay in that relationship with Christ, to bear no fruit, and be taken away. The key word is *abide* in Him. It is not enough to be joined to Christ initially; we must abide in Him in order to bear fruit. This parable also speaks to the question of "once saved, always saved." It shows that it is possible to be a branch but to be taken away.

To be joined to the Vine, Christ Jesus, is a beginning, but it's only the beginning. It is equally important to abide in Him. What does it mean to abide? If you do a word study in Scripture on the word *abide* you will discover its simple meaning is "to stay." When Jesus approached Emmaus with the two men on the day of the resurrection, He was invited to abide with them—stay with them. In the story of Zacchaeus, Jesus said, "To day I must abide at thy house." " 'I must stay in your house today' " (T.E.V.).

Abiding in the Vine does not take place automatically. The union with the Vine, the union with Christ, must be maintained. This parable gives great insight into the question of divine power and human effort in the Christian life. This was Jesus' treatise on how to use one's will and willpower in the ongoing Christian experience. We are to abide in Him and He in us. No branch will produce fruit if it is only occasionally connected to the Vine. The connection must be consistent. The branch must *abide* in the Vine.

A grapevine bears grapes because it is a grapevine, never in order to be one. A healthy branch will produce healthy fruit, naturally and spontaneously. If you have a healthy vine and a healthy branch connected to that vine, you *will* have fruit. If you do not want fruit from a branch, you can separate it from the vine, and nothing further need be done to prevent fruit. Fruit is one of the most spontaneous things that happens with a true vine and branches. If you want grapes, you don't try to produce grapes apart from the vine. Some people have tried. They have produced plastic grapes, and some of the plastic grapes look pretty good externally. But if you've ever tried a bite of one, you have found that it is very disappointing!

WHAT ARE THE GRAPES?

What do the grapes represent? Philippians 1:11: "Being filled with the fruits of righteousness, which are by Jesus Christ, unto the glory and praise of God." Please notice first of all that the fruits are fruits of righteousness; second, they are by Jesus Christ; and third, they are unto the praise and glory of God. And of course, Galatians 5:22, 23 speaks of the fruit of the Spirit: love, joy, peace, long-suffering, and so forth.

So, then, the fruit is righteousness—and righteousness is spontaneous for the branch that is connected to the True Vine. This means that the Christian never works hard on righteousness. He has never been asked to do that. Christ does not tell us to work hard on fruit—He invites us to abide in Him. So the deliberate effort in the Christian life is always and only toward fellowship with Jesus, toward abiding in the Vine. It is never toward producing the fruits of righteousness. For when we continue the connection with the Vine, the fruit will come.

Christ is the end of trying to produce fruit apart from the Vine. When we see our condition, see our total failure to produce real fruit apart from Him, then we can come to the place of admitting, with Paul, that the good that we try to perform we find not (Rom. 7:18). And not until then can we discover what it means to be truly connected with the Vine. Only then do we realize the necessity and privilege of abiding in Him.

"WITHOUT ME YE CAN DO NOTHING"

Some people are afraid of a do-nothing religion. But the words of John 15:5 are straight from Jesus' own lips. Notice them with a little different emphasis on the first phrase: *"I am* the vine, ye are the branches." I am the vine. You are not the vine. You are the branches. And "without me ye can do nothing." Please notice that although this is stated negatively, it can also be stated positively, as in Philippians 4:13: "I can do all things through Christ." With Him we can do all things.

As wonderful as salvation in heaven is, and as certain as our assurance of eternal life is, there is also the truth that Jesus can fulfill His purpose of living His life in us now as we submit to Him. And then He will bring forth much fruit. There is hope for a harvest, for produce, for results, in the Lord's vineyard. God Himself is interested in fruit. God Himself is eager to see results, to see a harvest. He is the husbandman, the great gardener, and a gardener hopes for results. He doesn't expect nothing.

Not too long ago I was discussing with one of my neighbors the finished work of Christ at the cross and how our salvation and our eternal life is assured because of the sacrifice of Jesus. Then he asked, "So what is the purpose of sanctification? What purpose is fulfilled by living the Christian life?"

Well, what is the purpose of fruit? It is for "the glory and praise of God.'' Matthew 5:16 says, "Let your light so shine before men, that they may see your good works, and glorify your Father which is in heaven.'' So what is the purpose of fruit? It is to glorify and honor God, and thus to reveal His love to others. We have, on the basis of Jesus' own teaching, the hope of a harvest, of fruit in the vineyard, for the glory of God.

HOW TO ABIDE

How do you abide in the Vine? How do you stay in this close connection with Jesus Christ? Once you have come to the end of your own resources, once you have realized your own inability to produce fruit apart from Him, once you recognize that without Him you can do nothing, what do you do? What does it mean to abide in Christ, to be in Christ, and have "Christ in you" (Col. 1:27)? Obviously this is referring to a very close relationship. That's what it's talking about. Christ is saying here, *Stay* in the relationship that was begun when you first accepted Me as your only hope. Stay in relationship with Me.

Please don't fall into the trap that we talked about earlier, of thinking that the way to stay in relationship with someone is by trying to do things to please him, to purchase his love with our deeds. The relationship produces the deeds, not the other way around. That is not the way we stay in relationship with anybody.

We accepted Jesus in the first place and became connected to the Vine, not by trying to produce deeds to make us worthy, but by accepting the mighty gift of His grace. However, let's not imply that accepting His grace has no effort attached to it, for most sinners have discovered that it is hard work to give up on themselves and come to Christ. But it is a different kind of work than working for righteousness and acceptance with God. The effort involved is in admitting, on a daily basis, that we can do nothing and in coming to Christ to accept His grace.

Have you ever found that coming to Christ on a daily basis is hard work? It is often that way. You'll have to admit that Paul used the right language when he called it a fight, "the good fight of faith" (1 Tim. 6:12). It isn't always easy to keep a corner of your day reserved for one-to-one communion with God. It isn't always natural to keep in touch with Him all through the day. Sometimes it takes real effort.

In John 15 Jesus tells us where the effort should be directed. He never asks us to work on producing fruit—He tells us to abide in Him. And if we choose to abide in Him, we have no choice on the fruit. It will be the natural and spontaneous result of that abiding.

We accept Jesus in the first place by faith in Him as our personal Saviour. That's how the union with the Vine is formed. That is also how it is continued. It is of utmost importance to realize that Jesus is not placing the responsibility of our works, or our fruit-bearing, upon us. While it is true that we *are* to bear fruit, it is also true that it is accomplished by faith alone in Him. "For without me, ye can do nothing." "The branch cannot bear fruit of itself, except it abide in the vine." But if it abide in the Vine it will bring forth much fruit. The fruit is the natural result of abiding in Christ.

BUT IT TAKES TIME

Now there's something else in this analogy of Jesus and the vineyard that we don't want to miss. That is, fruit doesn't happen overnight. The idea of a vine and branches and a vineyard all show that there is growth, progression. It happens little by little, not all at once. No vineyard is in a condition of perpetual harvest. Fruit takes time.

You may not be too familiar with working in a vineyard, but perhaps most of us have tried to transplant something. Let's go into the garden, instead of the vineyard, for just a moment as we notice this principle of growth. My wife brought a plant home from K Mart one day. For a while it did quite well in its bucket, but then it began to outgrow the bucket. So it needed to be transplanted. I picked a place at random, without her counsel, and put the plant there.

As a result of my planting it in the wrong place, I had to dig it up and transplant it again. And *I* didn't like it in that place, so I dug it up and transplanted it again. The plant is getting a little tired! About the time its roots begin to get enmeshed and fused with the soil, along comes this gardener and digs it up again. It's not doing too well—I noticed the leaves drooping on it the other day.

No, as you study the parable of the vineyard, you'll have to come to the realization that even when the branch stays connected with the vine, there is still a process of growth. This becomes very intriguing, because most of us are aware that even when we have chosen to stay with Christ, our immaturity is often demonstrated, and we are painfully aware that the job is not yet completed.

We also notice in the vineyard that it's not an on-again, off-again connection or partial dependence that enables the vine to bear fruit. It is not God's plan that we trust partly in Him and partly in ourselves.

We are reminded of the man in the olden days who was walking along a road with a pack on his back. Another man came by with a horse and buggy. The horse looked old and tired, the buggy looked a little small, and when the man with the pack on his back was invited aboard for a ride, he kept the pack on his back. He didn't think it would be fair to ask the driver and his horse to carry him and the pack, too!

Another man boarded a boat on the Mississippi River for a four-day journey. He bought a ticket, but it took all his money. He couldn't afford to pay extra for meals on board the ship, so he brought along some crackers and cheese to eat on the way. At each mealtime while the rest of the people would go to the dining room, he would hide behind a smokestack and eat his crackers and cheese. After a day or two his crackers and cheese began to get moldy, and he felt that he was about ready to starve to death. Then he was discovered in his hiding place and was told, "What's the matter with you, man? When you bought your ticket, you paid for all your meals as well. Come on and eat with the rest of us."

We accept God's grace and we say, That's marvelous. He has made provision to save me eternally in heaven. Now I must carry my own pack. And we exchange the burden of sin for the burden of holiness as we struggle to produce fruit in our own strength. Jesus has invited us to the marriage supper of the Lamb for fellowship with Him, and we think we have to bring our own food. We accept His mighty gospel as a gift and are thrilled with it, but the thrill dies out because we fail to see that in walking and fellowshiping with Him we are to work by the same method as when we first came to Him—all by faith. We keep wanting to add something to it, and so it becomes a painful process for us to allow Him to take our burdens, our sins, and our failures. We don't let Him give us the power for obedience that we so sadly lack. We don't realize that He wants to give us victory and overcoming as *gifts*.

JESUS, OUR EXAMPLE

There is another lesson we can learn from the vineyard parable, and that is the fact that Jesus is our example in abiding. Did you know that vines need support? Vines cannot stand alone, but must have the support of a trellis or some other mechanism. Jesus said that He was the vine, and His support came from His Father, who was the husbandman. In His life on earth Jesus became the greatest example of abiding and depending upon Another in personal fellowship and communication. We are told in Scripture of His arising a great while before day to go alone into nature for a time of communion with His Father. He often spent entire nights in prayer.

The idea of spending an entire night in prayer can be pretty awesome. But Jesus is not asking for that. His disciples weren't required to do that. But how long has it been since you spent fifteen minutes or half an hour responding to Jesus' loving invitation to abide in Him through personal fellowship?

I see two men walking along the trail toward Emmaus (Luke 24). A Stranger joins them. Their hearts burn within them as He talks to them on the way. It's late when they arrive at home, so they say to the Stranger, Abide with us. It's getting late. Stay at our house. They responded to Jesus even before they realized who the Stranger was.

My friend, it's getting late today. The signs all foretell that it's getting late. It's getting dark out there. It's always been dark, but it's getting even darker. Won't you join these two unsung disciples who chose to invite Jesus to abide with them? Won't you join them in saying to Him, Come and abide at our house?

THE COMING OF THE HARVEST

As we continue the abiding relationship with Christ, continue to allow Him to do His work in our lives, continue to seek for fellowship and communion with Him, we can look forward with joy to the time of the harvest. The time of harvest will come in our lives as we abide in Him. As His work is continued in us, the fruits of the Spirit will develop to maturity.

I had a friend who had a little girl who was 3 or 4 years old. My friend traveled a lot. One day he came back from a trip, and when he came into the house, the little girl, who hadn't seen him for several days, came running to him and said, "Daddy, look!

I've learned how to write." And she had a tablet with all kinds of scribbles and smudges and blotches all over it. It was a mess.

Like any good daddy he said, "Sure enough, you *did* learn to write. Isn't that wonderful? That's really good."

And he carried on so much about it that her eyes got big and her mouth dropped open and she said, "What does it say, Daddy?"

Then he went hot and cold. He didn't know what to say next. He stumbled for a moment or two, and then it came, and it must have come from above him. He sat down and said, "Here, Sweetheart, I'll tell you what it says. It says here that you are a little girl and that you really want to be able to write. It says you are trying hard to learn how to write. It also says that you are a growing little girl and someday you will write beautifully."

And she looked up and said, "Does it say all that, Daddy?"

"Yes."

I struggle as a growing Christian, and I produce my obedience, which is not real obedience at all. It's just like scribbles and blotches and smudges. And I take my obedience to God and I say, "Look! I've learned how to obey!"

And as my heavenly Father, He says, "Do you know what your efforts tell Me? They tell Me that you are a real Christian, that you really care. They say that you are growing, and someday you will know the real thing."

And so we can look forward to the time of maturity, of harvest, in our own lives, and we can also look forward to the time of harvest for the entire world. God is able to finish what He has begun in our lives. So long as we stay with Him we have nothing to fear.

There are millions of people today who believe in the second coming of Christ. There was a time when those who preached Christ's second advent were charged with being calamity howlers and prophets of doom. But today even scientists and statesmen who analyze world events are predicting disaster. Even secular leaders realize that this world is coming quickly to its end, and they are powerless to avert it.

Several years ago my father and my uncle were holding public meetings in a town. My uncle had just started preaching one night about the end of the world and the second coming of Jesus when a man jumped up right near the front. He turned around and began shouting at the congregation, "Don't believe what these Venden brothers are saying. They are just a couple of calamity howlers come to town to deceive you. They're talking about the end of the world, and it's never going to happen. Things continue just like they always have, and always will." And he turned to my uncle and said, "You can't show me one single proof that it's going to happen!"

And my uncle said, "Yes, I can! You're the latest one I've seen."

The man said, "What do you mean?"

My uncle turned the pages in his Bible and read from 2 Peter 3:3, 4: "There shall come in the last days scoffers, walking after their own lusts, and saying, Where is the promise of his coming? for since the fathers fell asleep, all things continue as they were from the beginning of the creation."

And the man slumped into his seat. Exciting things happened back there on the sawdust trail! The Lord gave the right scripture at the right time.

God doesn't start something and then leave it unfinished. When He begins a thing, He sees it through to the end. Even when Jesus left the tomb on the morning of the resurrection, He paused long enough to fold the grave clothes and neatly put them down. He was finished with them. He needed them no more. And how much more surely will He finish the great plan of redemption, of restoration. He has made provision to more than make up to us for being born into this world of sin. Aren't you thankful that He is able to follow through on His plan of salvation, clear through to the end, which is only the beginning of eternity? Nothing can deter him.

SECOND COMING: GOOD NEWS OR BAD NEWS?

What is your reaction when you read or hear or think of the second coming of Christ? Does it seem like good news, or bad news? Are you excited? or scared? The crucial question is Are *you* going to be ready? "Oh," you may say, "I'm too far from it. I'll never make it. There's not a chance in the world for me." I asked a young man what would be the first thing he'd want to do in heaven. He replied, "If I got to heaven, I'd be so surprised I don't know what I'd do!"

That's why I'd like to bring you a text that speaks hope to each one, because it tells how we can be ready for Christ's coming. Ephesians 2:13: "But now in Christ Jesus ye who sometimes were far off are made nigh by the blood of Christ." Do you feel that you are a long way off? Through Jesus' blood, through His atonement and sacrifice at the cross for you, you are made near. And that's good news, isn't it? Salvation is not something we earn; it is something we receive as a gift. And we can receive it anew every day.

Are you saved? Can you know that you are saved now? Well, it depends on what you mean. There are three Greek words for *salvation*. One relates to the question "Have I accepted the death of Jesus for all mankind?" Another, "Am I presently in a saving relationship with Jesus?" And a third, "Will I be saved at some time in the future?"

Let me ask you: Have you accepted the death of Jesus for all mankind? Then you are saved in that sense. Are you presently in a saving relationship with Jesus Christ? Are you on speaking terms with Him? Did you talk to Him today? Did you spend time with Him personally? You ought to be able to know the answer to that question. And we don't have to worry about whether or not we will be saved at some future time. We cannot predict what we may decide in the meantime. But we can know that we are saved today. And we can continue to choose God today. That is the big issue. Have you accepted Jesus and His blood today, which brings you close to heaven? You can make that choice.

And as you continue to make that choice, you can look forward with joy to the end of sin, to the time when Jesus comes again for His people.

KNOWING GOD = LIFE ETERNAL

Jesus said in John 17:3, "And this *is* life eternal, that they might know thee the only true God, and Jesus Christ, whom thou hast sent." The entire basis of the Christian life is in knowing God. This is the avenue by which we accept His salvation, His forgiveness, His power. And knowing God or not knowing God becomes the crucial issue at the end. Notice how it happens.

When Jesus comes again, there will be two groups of people. They are called by different names—the good and the bad, the righteous and the wicked, the sheep and the goats, the just and the unjust, the wheat and the tares, the wise and the foolish, the hot and the cold, and so on. But there are only two groups when Jesus comes again.

In Day 1 we studied a story about a wedding recorded in Matthew 25. There were five wise bridesmaids and five foolish. And Jesus gave us insight as to what determined the difference between the two groups. When the foolish girls came to seek admission to the wedding banquet, the answer was given to them, "I know you not." In Matthew 7, the same division is described. Verses 22, 23: "Many will say to me in that day, Lord, Lord, have we not prophesied in thy name? and in thy name have cast out devils? and in thy name done many wonderful works? And then will I profess unto them, *I never knew you:* depart from me, ye that work iniquity.''

From these scriptures we can see that there will be only two classes of people at the very end—those who know God, and those who don't know God. There will be no other option.

But let's add to this another scripture, found in Revelation 3. The first three chapters of the book of Revelation tell about seven churches. Chapter 3, verse 13 and onward, describes the last of these seven churches in the history of churches up until shortly before Jesus comes. The last church is known as Laodicea. ''He that hath an ear, let him hear what the Spirit saith unto the churches. Unto the angel of the church of the Laodiceans write; These things saith the Amen, the faithful and true witness, the beginning of the creation of God.'' Who is that? That's Jesus.

And don't forget that Revelation is Jesus' own book. The Gospels are written about Jesus, but they are not Jesus' own books. But Revelation is the only book that starts out with ''The Revelation of Jesus Christ, which . . . he sent . . . unto his servant John.'' Of all the Bible books Revelation is Jesus' book in a unique way. So it ought to be of supreme interest to those who are interested in Jesus.

Then comes the description of the church known as Laodicea. Verse 15: ''I know thy works, that thou art neither cold nor hot: I would thou wert cold or hot.'' Wait a minute! That's a startling thought. Would God rather have people cold than lukewarm? That's what it says. Verse 16: ''So then because thou art lukewarm, and neither cold nor hot, I will spue thee out of my mouth.'' That's another way of saying that lukewarm people make God sick! ''Because thou sayest, I am rich, and increased with goods, and have need of nothing; and knowest not that thou art wretched, and miserable, and poor, and blind, and naked'' (verse 17). So there you have the description of Laodicea, the lukewarm church.

WHAT *IS* LUKEWARM?

Now if Laodicea is known for being lukewarm, what percentage of people do you suppose would be lukewarm? The majority would have to be lukewarm if it's known for being lukewarm, right? That's logical. When we say that America is a democracy, what do we mean by that? We mean that the majority of people in America believe in a democratic form of government. So at least 51 percent of the people in Laodicea would be lukewarm. And that's a pretty heavy statement right there, isn't it? That means that the church up until shortly before Jesus comes will have a lot of lukewarm people in it.

If the majority of people in the church are lukewarm, you could expect to have some lukewarm teachers, couldn't you? You could expect some lukewarm pastors and leaders and administrators. I mean, the lukewarm are likely to put into office some of their own, aren't they? You would find lukewarmness permeating everywhere, because the majority of people in the church of Laodicea are lukewarm.

That leads us to another question. What *is* lukewarm? What makes a person lukewarm? I sometimes use an old illustration that has to do with the kitchen sink—a little lesson in home economics. You have a single spigot on the sink, and a handle on the left for hot, and one on the right for cold. If you want to get lukewarm, what do you do? You turn on equal parts of cold and hot, and you get lukewarm.

This illustration may not help a whole lot, because it would be ridiculous to think of a Laodicean person as one who is cold on the right side and hot on the left side. But it does give a clue that lukewarm is somehow a combination, or mixture, of hot and cold.

If we let Scripture interpret itself, we discover what it is that makes a lukewarm person. Read it for yourself in Matthew 23, where Jesus made it very clear that the problem of the people in the days when He was here was that they were hot on the outside but cold on the inside. That's what makes a lukewarm person. Jesus said, "You people are like whited sepulchres that you go out and whitewash every spring. You look good on the outside, but inside you are full of dead men's bones." In other words, they were rotten on the inside. That was pretty strong language, right? Jesus went so far, in Matthew 23, as to call them " 'snakes and sons of snakes!' " (verse 33, T.E.V.). Yet He had tears in His voice as He said it.

In the same chapter He said, "You hypocrites. You clean the outside of the cup. What you should do is clean the inside of the cup, and the outside will be clean as well." If the inside is right, the outside will be right too. But it is possible for the outside to look right and the inside to be rotten still. A person can look good on the outside and go through all the right motions and perform all the right behavior and be simply a moral person. Morality has to do primarily with outside, external conformity to the laws and rules and regulations. The moral person follows the mores of his society on the outside, but inside he may be just the opposite. So a lukewarm person is one who does all the right things but for all the wrong reasons.

The majority of people in the church up until shortly before Jesus comes are externalists. They are trying to do what's right on the outside, trying to get righteousness by works. They do not know God, yet they try to live as His children. And the pitful thing is that Laodicea doesn't even know its condition. It doesn't know. It is "wretched, and miserable, and poor, and blind, and naked," and knows it not.

But wait a minute—when Jesus actually comes again, how many groups of people will there be? We've already noticed that there are going to be only two groups of people when Jesus comes again. Who are they? They are the hot and the cold. When Jesus comes again, bringing His reward with Him, there are only two groups of people. There will be no lukewarm reward for the lukewarm. There is no lukewarm lake of fire for the lukewarm. There is no lukewarm heaven for the lukewarm.

So if there are only two groups of people when Jesus returns, then the next question would be What happens to the large group of lukewarm people? They disappear. Where do they go? They go either hot or cold. That means that from the time of Laodicea, the last of the seven churches of Revelation, until the time that Jesus actually comes, there is an interim when people go one way or the other. There is a polarization that takes place, and nobody remains lukewarm any longer.

SIGN OF CHRIST'S COMING

Now the reason I am interested in this subject is that I believe this polarization has been happening for several years already and is becoming more pronounced every day. I believe that this is the greatest single sign that Jesus' coming is right upon us. The evidence is that immediately before Jesus' coming, people are going to be divided into two groups, only two groups, the hot and the cold.

With that in mind, let's read Revelation 3:18, 19. Here is the counsel to the people who are in Laodicea and who are lukewarm. "I counsel thee to buy of me gold tried in the fire, that thou mayest be rich; and white raiment, that thou mayest be clothed, and that the shame of thy nakedness do not appear; and anoint thine eyes with eyesalve, that thou mayest see. As many as I love, I rebuke and chasten: be zealous therefore, and repent."

Let's break this message to the lukewarm down into two parts, for the sake of our understanding. The first part is verses

15-17. It's the *rebuke* to Laodicea. I know your works; you are neither cold nor hot. I wish you were either cold or hot. But you say you are rich, increased with goods, and have need of nothing, and don't know that you're wretched and miserable and poor and blind and naked. That's the rebuke to Laodicea.

Now there's something beautiful about God's patience in relationship to His church. It's nice to know that even Laodicea, a lukewarm body, can still be His church. He must be very patient. But God never rebukes people without giving them help. So the second part of the message to these Laodiceans is *counsel*. "I counsel thee to buy of me gold tried in the fire, that thou mayest be rich; and white raiment, that thou mayest be clothed . . . ; and . . . eyesalve, that thou mayest see."

So the second part, verse 18, is the counsel to the Laodiceans. The first part is the rebuke, and the second part is the counsel.

Let's take a minute to get together on what the counsel is all about. Those who have studied the symbolism in Revelation tell us that gold represents faith and love. And white raiment—what is that? It's the righteousness of Christ. And eyesalve indicates spiritual discernment, insight—which comes through the Holy Spirit. So the counsel to the Laodiceans, the lukewarm people, is that they need the righteousness of Christ by faith, which brings love and is accomplished through the Holy Spirit. The counsel to the Laodiceans is their need of the righteousness of Christ by faith, and faith comes only by a daily, personal, one-to-one relationship with Jesus.

THE RESULTS OF THE COUNSEL

What will be the result of this counsel of the True Witness? It will be the thing that will cause the third group, the lukewarm group, to disappear, to go either hot or cold.

Now it's easy to see that a rebuke could cause some

polarization. It's possible to get up and give some scathing rebuke, cry aloud and spare not, really let people have it for their sins, and split churches right down the middle. But there is one thing for sure—*revival* has never happened on the basis of externals. Never! External change may be called reformation, but reformation is no good unless it is preceded by revival. It's the revial that brings genuine reformation, and revival has to do with the heart, with the inward spiritual life.

So we have to underscore it carefully here that any time we have genuine spiritual revival, it is going to be based on the righteousness of Christ, and faith and love and the Holy Spirit and the one-to-one fellowship with Jesus.

But Revelation 3 indicates that this message is the great dividing message: it causes people to polarize into either of two groups—hot or cold. What is there about the message of the righteousness of Christ by faith and the need for the relationship with Christ that causes people to go one way or the other?

There's only one answer. Laodiceans, lukewarm people, have gotten used to finding their security in something other than the righteousness of Christ, and faith and love and the Holy Spirit. They have found their security in the external things they have been doing. Strong people can find security in externals, because strong people can live good moral lives on the outside. They say, Don't bother me with the righteousness of Christ by faith and with my need for a one-to-one relationship with God to receive His faith and love. I'm living a good moral life. God, You keep Your planets from running into one another, and help the drunk in the gutter and the harlots and the thieves. But me? I'm getting along fine, thank You.

That's the problem of the Laodicean, the lukewarm person. That was the problem of the externalists in the days of Jesus. When Jesus came along and talked about God and faith and love and surrender, it was a threat to their security. It pulled the rug out from underneath them. And the person who has been thinking that he has assurance of heaven someday because he is living a good life cannot stay the same when he hears the emphasis upon the righteousness of Christ as our only hope. Either he will welcome it as good news and enter into the faith relationship with Christ, accepting of His righteousness and love on a day-by-day basis, or he will walk away from the whole package and say, "No, thanks, I'm not interested." It's a mystery that is hard to explain.

But wherever Jesus went, people never remained the same. Wherever Jesus is uplifted, there's either a revival or a riot. Wherever the apostle Paul went, determined to know nothing except Jesus and Him crucified, people went one way or the other. Either they welcomed him into their synagogues, or they ran him out of town. There is no possibility of straddling the fence in the presence of Jesus.

So this is what causes the large middle group to disappear just shortly before Jesus returns. At the time of His coming there will be only two groups. This emphasis upon the righteousness of Christ by faith alone has been rising steadily, and nothing is stopping it. It's the last message just before Jesus returns, and it causes the last events just before He comes again. We can rejoice when we see it happening, for it tells us that Jesus' coming is very, very near.

THE GREAT DIVIDE

This great divide is going on right now. It is happening in every church, it is happening in the world at large. Jesus said, I am not come to send peace, but a sword (Matt. 10:34). He talks about relatives ending up being against one another. And this is also being seen today. For years it has been possible for two people to live together as husband and wife under the same roof and be very compatible because they were both lukewarm. But as lukewarm people disappear shortly before Jesus comes, sometimes one goes hot and the other goes cold. And what happens in the home? There is incompatibility, isn't there?

Did you know that the divorce rate in the United States is something like 53 percent of the marriage rate? Did you know that the divorce rate among church members is basically the same? It didn't used to be that way, not at all. So we have all kinds of results as the polarization goes down the center of families, down the center of churches. People are going one way or the other, and it's happening fast.

I am willing to take the risk of saying that every one of us knows today which way we are going, right now. How can we know? As we have noticed, it's determined on the basis of knowing God or not knowing God. We could boil it down to one question: Do you know Jesus as your personal friend? Are you spending time with Him, one to one, continuing to accept His saving grace? That's the vital question.

You may be going through real, agonizing struggles, but if you know Jesus on a personal basis day by day, you're going to be on the winning side. And even though we may lose an occasional battle, God has already won the war. If you've read the end of the Book, you know we're going to win!

John 17:3 says it so clearly: "This is life eternal, that they might know thee the only true God, and Jesus Christ, whom thou hast sent." It is in knowing Jesus that our salvation is received and continued to the end, which is only the beginning!